Jean Giono

# OCCUPATION
# JOURNAL

Translated from the French by Jody Gladding

*archipelago books*

First published as *Journal de l'Occupation* by Editions Gallimard, Paris, 1995

Archipelago Books
232 Third St. #A111
Brooklyn, NY 11215
www.archipelagobooks.org

Library of Congress Cataloging-in-Publication Data
available upon request

Distributed by Penguin Random House
www.penguinrandomhouse.com

Cover art: *Poplars* by Georges Seurat

This book was made possible by the New York State Council on the Arts with the
support of Governor Andrew M. Cuomo and the New York State Legislature.

This work received support from the French Ministry of Foreign Affairs
and the Cultural Services of the French Embassy in the United States
through their publishing assistance program.

Funding for the translation of this book was provided by a grant
from the Carl Lesnor Family Foundation.

Archipelago Books also gratefully acknowledges the generous support
of the National Endowment for the Arts, Lannan Foundation,
the Nimick Forbesway Foundation, the Centre National du Livre,
and the New York City Department of Cultural Affairs.

PRINTED IN THE USA

# OCCUPATION
# JOURNAL

# 1943

*September 20*

There is such confusion in people's minds that, even among the best of my acquaintances, no one knows how to conduct himself according to the simple rules of nobility and grandeur anymore. In the fellowship of the Contadour, R.B. was a comrade who seemed to me capable of understanding and applying those rules on all occasions. He was clear-sighted and bright, and if it worried me knowing that he regularly spent time with reserve officers, I imagined that his social position demanded it (teaching at the teachers' college). His convictions, if he was expressing them honestly, were pacifist and humane. He could not retain his integrity in the tangle of propaganda. It's hard for me to imagine that this is the same man now mixed up in arms drops, who runs off and distributes machine guns to young men hidden in his county. I know – if I take into account the terrible worries eating at his heart – (his love for M., his crazy son) there are certainly excuses for his desire to escape at any cost his life's inconceivable misery. All the same, I was hoping he would escape in the direction of nobility.

In our modern mechanical world, it's clearly very tempting to embrace the cause of a religious war. It must give one the impression, despite everything, that he is a thinking being. And, after the fate dealt to man in 1930–1940, it must suddenly be so invigorating that it's difficult to resist. But the quest for the Grail made the knights-errant gallop in a straight line. Even Don Quixote walks straight. Today it seems as though the Grail has shattered and they are chasing all the scattered bits of it in every direction. They charge blindly, noses in the air, radios behind them in the saddle, newspaper helmets fastened securely on their skulls. Those who have donned secret papers, clandestine publications, think they are wearing the most magical helmets of all. Not a single head remains bare. For my part, I consider it important above all not to be duped. That's what I peacefully strive for. I know the deep wretchedness of our generation and the ones that follow, and I have tried, with what means I have, to provide a small cure. I recognize that I can do nothing. Lacking either enough intelligence for problems that are too great or enough simplicity for problems that are so hugely simple they defy mathematics, I would nevertheless reserve the right to laugh and comfort myself with scorn, *precisely* applied. English generosity; American civilization.

Last week, there was an assassination attempt here against the head of the militia. He was returning from the cinema with his family when an armed stranger shot at him. Ch. shot back and killed his assailant. At which point a sort of impromptu legend started. The assailant, who had come from Marseille to kill Ch. (it seems he confessed before dying), was a miner from the north of France, his children had been killed in a bombardment, and his wife, I don't know what, something terrible, I dare say, no doubt raped by the Uhlans. He became the hero. Almost everyone attended his funeral, Dr. G. and his wife prominently at the head of the line. Dr. G. is a perfect and pure careerist, an opportunist, an ambitious man who dreams of a seat on the district council. That's clear to everyone here. But he was much admired behind the hearse. Of course Dr. G. is not a Communist, he made two or three million in a few years (he arrived here very poor), and is an admirable specimen of the ordinary materialist. He's only trying to position himself for the next wave of "honors." That's nothing. It's only that no one thought to explain this in a simple way. The man from Marseille was really only a paid assassin. Because why – even as martyr and hero – especially as hero – why come to assassinate Ch.? The back wheel of the wagon. Ch. is not exactly anyone important. At present, it's simply personal accounts being settled. And personal business being conducted (Dr. G.). All that is fine, I'm not asking Dr. G. or the assassin or Ch. to be Lancelot of the Lake or Percival, I only ask that no one tries to make me believe they are.

Wonderful weather, exhilarating wind coming from the sheep plateaus. Cool and crisp, and those earth tones and bruised sky that announce autumn. The sound of the bell that rings at noon undulates in the wind like a cracked whip. The air is delicious to breathe. I am going to start writing again. These days. I need a serious discipline for mind and body.

Plans for *Fragments d'un paradis*. Never forgetting that after *Don Quixote* (I must begin the discussion with myself on this book. In Doré's illustrations, Don Quixote resembles my beloved father, but embittered. My father was good and gentle, clearly readable in his entire body), never forgetting that Cervantes finished his life writing the *The Trials of Persiles and Sigismunda*. I am anxious for Jacinto G. to send me this book in Spanish; I'm going to try to learn enough Spanish to read it.

*Fragments* must be an adieu to the poetic (as *Don Quixote* is an adieu to *grandeur* – and not a satire on chivalry. What pettiness! Imagine Cervantes wanting to mock chivalry! And he would finish his life writing (with the most careful attention to the form and spirit of it) a novel of Chivalry! No, he wanted to say a melancholy farewell (hence Don Quixote's madness) to grandeur). *Fragments* must say farewell to the poetic, to lyricism, to the "lie" without which there is no art, by which I mean the subjective. Goodbye to romanticism, on the threshold of 1616, when truth, exactitude, the slice of life will be extolled (you'll see) (but Maupassant was lying (was interpreting), but Gide lies (happily), but Eugène Dabit suffered and died for not knowing how to lie, that is, for not having the strength (first of all, the physical strength) to stomach "spectacles" in order to express them in the end as Van Gogh expresses a wheat field and a cypress. Because they know and he knew what it is that interests me, which is not the cypress or the wheat field. It is the cypress + Van Gogh and the wheat field + Van Gogh. The mark. To leave his mark). Because how could he have been in step with Communist times?

Finishing the third act of *Voyage* without proving anything. Having wanted to demonstrate a slowing of the action in the second part of Act I, an act I am not at all happy with.

Writing the text for *Virgil* that Corrêa wants and immediately afterwards (before the end of the year if possible), I hope to begin *Fragments*. Because if I wrote *Le Voyage* for the theater, it's so that I might finally have a little peace financially (I must speak a little about my legend one of these days, and in particular about my "wealth" (in 1940, living on 20,000 for the whole year, nine people, and actually giving the figures) because what Vlaminck says about me he says relying on legend alone, journalistic and cinematographic legend). (I am not suspicious enough of visitors. Too nice.) Tino Rossi aside, of course. Because he's not completely wrong. There is a little of that. But I believe – I may be wrong. I don't dispute it. I believe that's all there is. Writing *Fragments* for my own pleasure, as I like, at my own pace (which is slow), taking the most pleasure possible in the writing.

Yesterday evening, Uncle did not return. Believed it to be the usual fit of drunkenness and expected to hear the doorbell during the night. This morning I realized that he had still not come home. It was Charles I heard having coffee. I wondered if Uncle might be dead in the pavilion, a stroke or from hanging himself. Suicide is a possibility with this hideous, horrible, arrogant, worthless but sensitive man who has turned everyone against him. Has made everyone detest him, even his own daughters, and yet, sometimes, a burst of grandeur, I thought to myself… this morning I went to see, to have a look in the pavilion with its door left open. I looked in the linden tree. Charles had the same thought. My mother, too. Charles went to look out the windows.

He was not there, he told me. Then, later, while I was writing, I heard him coughing and clearing his throat below in the garden. He'd only gone on his usual binge. Too often (always) I judge others according to myself. I believe that's what happened over the twenty years with Lucien Jacques as well.

*September 21*

Jean B., who spent two days here with his wife and his son M., visibly bristled or didn't respond when I openly expressed all my contempt for the small thinkers of the era who have earned their degrees listening to the radio. He remained very good and fine, an excellent gentleman (which he is) but I recognized some reproach, not in his eyes, nor in the creases of his mouth, but in the fixed lines of his face. They said clearly that he did not dare contradict me but that he did not agree with me. Marthe watched him from the corner of her eye. His daughter Jacqueline has a marvelous a mind, she has chosen a wonderful occupation. She's passionate about pottery and at the moment lives with potters outside Bourges, in the manner of great artists of the Renaissance. And I believe with all my heart that she possesses the wonderful truth that, if understood by a greater number, could itself alone create a Renaissance – for everything, for art as well as for life. She lives a magnificent life, making her passion her occupation, tracking down the artisans' secrets, the mystery of the glaze, the good – or bad – fortunes of the kiln (she already understands why it must be wood-fired instead of electric). And this is exactly the opposite of Industry and the Commune. It belongs to Art and to Individuality. And Jean B. understands and admires the mind and the work of his daughter. Hence this confusion. Because what I'm defending, precisely, is Jacqueline, my dear old Jean. I said that to him. I'm sure he did not understand. He encourages his daughter to construct a world that he himself destroys. That makes him like the pacifist Robert B., machine gun dealer and certified promoter of the war of 1960. With this category of the damned, the only relationships possible anymore are those of Dante.

We are in a religious war. After defeat, the French ought to have thought their way through to building a future and paths to a future by which the victor would disappear or else serve the vanquished. We ought to have responded to material victory by rising above our victors spiritually, and above what we ourselves had been, instead of wanting to be victor in turn (the chain of wars). That ought to have been the moment of great visions. But there were no fertile minds. No one is capable anymore of seeing the great beasts that rise from the fields, trees, and oceans. Among those preparing future woes, there are some of good faith who imagine they are saving the world and cooking up happiness. But they put all their trust in the *material*. As if the *material* will win the war. From every side the material kills the heroic. And if I rejoice in the death of military heroism (it survives only in aviation – dive bombing – just flying bombers is no longer heroic enough anymore. Which explains youth's infatuation with flying. The last chance for the *knight*. They feel a connection with the *last romanticism* there, a final place for the *individual*. So very instructive is repugnance for community), I regret the death of heroism pure and simple. It was the highest poetry man could attain. And modern man is going to die from a poetry hemorrhage. (Poetry is what Jacqueline B. desperately seeks. It is why her father's heart exalts when he considers what she does. But he defeats it and renders it impossible by his thoughts and actions. Thinking corrupted by parties, by the passion of parties.) They think they inhabit a world in which everything is reduced to the material. They don't realize that material itself, the most dense material, is more insubstantial and porous than a sponge, and like a sponge at the very depths of the sea, it is bathed, permeated, swollen, enlivened by the spirit and by salty mysteries that, from one moment to the next, can seethe with unpredictable typhoons. They are not yet far enough beyond their depths to notice that a train wheel or a blast furnace *does not float* (try to create something that floats. From there: *Fragments*).

*September 22*

*The art of war.* In the course of an otherwise heated conversation with Auguste M., he said to me, "What thrills me is to see Australian shepherds on the battlefield defeating the most scientific army and the generals of the most *artistic* school of war of all times." It is true and thrills me as well. There is no art of war. But I'm afraid that this absence of art, this *ease*, makes it all the more tempting. If everyone can make war with some chance of success, if it's *within everyone's reach*, I'm afraid the desire for it will become irresistible. Everything points to its lack of grandeur: its ease, its use of lies, treachery, contempt for the given word, "the end justifies the means," the death of heroism; there is not even national interest, no one is defending his country any longer. This is expressed and explained every day loud and clear, but there are none so deaf as those who will not hear. No one hates the war. They hate the enemy, they hate those who may threaten their wealth, but they do not hate the war. And no horror will make them hate it. Neither the reduction of

Hamburg to embers nor the destruction of Coventry troubles anyone's sleep. If London or Berlin were destroyed tomorrow, no one's digestive system would stop. It is only a matter of brief news items; you cannot make an omelet without breaking the eggs, and everyone's self-interest is protected by that omelet. But when it happens to your own eggs, then you roar, then you curse the heavens, and you are so surprised.

Everyone rejoiced yesterday over the battles of Corsica. The war is now no more than a hundred kilometers away.

Autumn arrived early this year. It's here. The mellow sound of the fountain in the silent fog. Peace! And the first shiver that makes the warmth of wool sweaters and the inside of houses seem magnificent. It's getting dark earlier.

*September 23*

Just received a letter from Z. A very beautiful letter, completely calm, because it concerns his native country with its incomparable beauty and peace. It includes excerpts from a letter from his sister on the Paris bombardment: "The whole city witnessed the air strike, the D.C.A. firing as ever. As for me, I saw three planes descend in flames and only three parachutes opened and the whole descent had an appalling slowness about it against a beautiful blue sky, a magnificent sun. Squadrons continued to pass regularly through the fire and we thought that, apart from the bombs dropped from planes nearby, Paris would not be targeted. Then a deluge of bombs on Paris unleashed panic and half the city disappeared in an opaque black cloud, impenetrable because it was full of blinding shards of metal. You could not see ten meters. A.'s hotel was completely reduced to rubble."

Further on in Z.'s letter and concerning his own country: "The country is all abuzz with conspiracies, Gaullist and non-Gaullist meetings. The bawlers bawl, the moaners moan, they kill each other over a yes or a no, they stoke the hell fires *while losing nothing of their petit bourgeois air* (the emphasis mine). No one is surprised anymore, it is nothing that in the last month a militia leader and another landowner were KILLED (the emphasis Z.'s) here. They are buried and it's on to the next one.

"That sums up the current times, as much in Paris as in N. It is very much the Middle Ages of the *Fall of Constantinople*, foreseen in 1939. So when 'will the white gathering swell'?"

*September 24*

It's impossible for me not to be disturbed by the idea that others form of me through the journalists' legend. If I make a show of indifference, that's just what I do. Nevertheless, as it would be useless to contradict it – and how could I anyway – I imagine what counts is the work. I know perfectly well that this is small consolation, and how the work itself can be distorted, but if it makes the time pass, it will make the rest pass as well. And if I projected the exact image of what I am, would there be the least gain, I mean, in the beauty of living? Aside from a taste of being appreciated, or not, according to my true value, I don't see how that would benefit me. That men like Joset (and I name him so this proper noun can serve as common noun for others like him) are no longer my friends neither provides or costs me anything. I even have the feeling that Henri Fluchère's shortcomings, for example, shed some light on the rather "gentleman-like" situation that was established between us in the guise of friendship. We had not been friends in school, as I was older than he was, and then he left for Cambridge. He only courted me after I emerged from bank employment, after *Colline* and what they called fame (created by the newspapers). Basically, I think he held it against me for succeeding instead of him. I would truly like to be wrong because I loved him. I entrusted him with the translation of *Le Chant du monde* at a critical moment in his life when he needed to believe in his own worth. Not to mention, I gave him more than his due in the Heubsch contract since it involved us both. I gave him an equal share (this mania for always rejecting the higher position when it's mine, how can anyone believe in me after that?). From that alone, he has now earned a tidy sum in dollars from Viking Press. Faithfully supported him in the Denise Clairouin attack, remaining faithfully at his side. I have real affection for him. What are his shortcomings? In addition to what I just said, his lack of critical judgment in the face of rumors.

Or maybe – and deep in my heart this is what I want – I'm the one who is the bastard and there's nothing in what I say, and he's not letting himself be taken for a ride by the Krivines and he's my faithful friend and it's really me who is ignoble and he no longer comes to see me simply because he no longer comes to see me, that's all.

I have never been so happy as now. Never have the books been so delicious. Never has love been so peaceful, so vivid, so fantastic. Never have the days been so wonderfully harmonious. Never have I worked so patiently. Never have I been so wonderfully intent on my riches. Could it be that the end is approaching?

Extraordinary fall of the rebel angels, the fallen friends, even to the point that Lucien Jacques's withdrawal sheds light on all the extraordinary generosity that has exhausted me. Maybe my peace comes from no longer having to provide for anyone.

In Epting's preface to the *Anthology of German Poetry* that I received, I read: "There are others (poets) who have been deliberately excluded even though the French literati may expect to find them here. It was a matter of applying the principles that have come to light in Germany over the course of the last ten years and that have illuminated the true German spiritual tradition. For a long time now, the way French literary circles represent that tradition has not corresponded to the way it is conceived in Germany…"

I beg your pardon, Monsieur Epting. This is no longer the anthology of all German poetry but of *a* German poetry, and thus you're the exact opposite of that good apostle you claim to be. How would you like us to approach this? I want to be able to hear Jewish songs and Communist songs if they are beautiful, and if they represent Germany as well. What can I do with this selection of poets? It is so politically determined that it ruins Hölderin and Novalis for me. And I keep wanting to say to myself, "But the most beautiful was forgotten" – worse: "the most beautiful was rejected." That's not true, but what a blunder to leave such an opening for suspicion and retort. But it's our fine lack of generosity on display once again and what stupid things it makes us do. (Generosity again, as I wrote at the beginning of today's note) If there are very good poets opposed to National-Socialism, well, Monsieur Epting, you need to include them. If there is very beautiful poetry opposing your *true* tradition, that's because your *true* tradition is not entirely true. You cannot make truly beautiful poetry not exist, no matter where it comes from, and Boris Pilniak is a great Russian poet nevertheless. When it's a matter of scorning poets, that's easy, but really how frightened you are of them, and consequently you want to *dictate*.

I'm not being fair. Lucien gave me so many things. Certainly more than I credit him for. He was the first to believe in me, and he was faithful to me for twenty years. And perhaps Henri Fluchère is also a wonderful friend.

*September 25*

Yet another example of misguided zeal. After all this, I admit it's difficult to regard me as sane. From the beginning, I was against that film Régnier tried to make about me. Nothing offends me more and nothing is less like me than that representation; nevertheless it exists and it's true that I finally did give in. But I gave in to Régnier's insistence, his need for a leg up (and he's done well with this film, which has brought in some capital). He must admit that I advised him several times not to have me appear. I reduced my presence to a minimum. I refused to speak (for which Meiffret reproaches me), as much as I could, I cut scenes in which he wanted me to act; I'm only seen walking and writing, which is how I practice my occupation. But I agree that it's still too much and should not have appeared. That was my ardent wish. I asked nothing. My mistake was agreeing and I agreed only to help Régnier. If this film were seen clearly, only humility and not a bit of pride would be apparent there. I never considered that it would have to be protected from serving other people's purposes. But of course the viewer is not obligated to look beyond the screen. And I'm the one in the wrong.

Thunderstorms. A beautiful autumn. Sky inhabited by giant clouds. A very long southern wind. Extremely slow gestures from the storm, thunder like syrup that doesn't clap but collapses. Élise, who is obsessed with the thought of the *noise* of battle, and the girls sometimes think it's gunfire. Basically, what's important is to live, not the idea that others form of our lives. One must try to write, to create, above the whole legend. If I can't do that, too bad, I will have tried and that will have been interesting. The arrival of the storm's great darkness is very sweet to my heart.

An hour after having written that note, lightning suddenly flashed through my office at the top of the house. A small pink pinpoint of light and a crackling near the window. Dumbfounded I just had time to say Oh! before the thunder clapped. Élise, who was napping below, ran out of her room, hands over her ears. That was ten minutes ago and my back and head ache. As though there was a heavy iron crown around my head. Up to that moment, the rumbling was very far off, then suddenly, a huge thunderclap. That's why I think the lightning came in through the window and escaped through the chimney. I was lying on my divan to read Hoffmann. Weakness in my elbows and knees now, and my head not exactly aching, but "funny." As if it were wood. I am writing this by the window and at the least noise, instinctively (absolutely instinctively) I shrink away from it, recoiling as if I expected to be clawed.

*September 26*

I am still quite dumbfounded by yesterday afternoon's lightning. It was really very tiny and the effect on the body very strange. So sudden that the mind did not have time to function; nevertheless, in that absolute silence, I understood everything. It was precisely, I believe, *divine*, that is, the knowledge of things before they happen. I was on the other side of the event, *on the wooden side of the arrow*. That lasted a quarter of a second, but I will never forget that quarter second, during which I was *released from all dimensions* and conscious to a degree that cannot be expressed.

If that could last a few seconds or a minute, I believe that many mysteries would be clarified. Knowledge of a tangential world.

This morning gunfire can be heard very distinctly from the south. Then calm, a cool wind, clear sky, bright sunshine, and it's a beautiful Sunday.

Music with Meyerowitz this afternoon. He wanted me to hear Offenbach's *La Grande-Duchesse de Gérolstein*, devilishly anti-militarist. More depth than Rossini but less brilliance. Then Prelude and Fugue in C sharp minor in which, in the fugue, the phrase sometimes occurs *in reverse* and extends the harmony. That suddenly produces a very deep recognition. Then Prelude and Fugue in G major (1st volume *Well-tempered Klavier*), Brahms's Intermezzo in E flat minor op. 118, no. 6. Physical pain. Cancer. Tropic of Cancer.

A shapeless sky this evening as after the mistral sometimes. It's cold and the sky is particularly apocalyptic. The coming night is truly like a lead weight. Just now some artillery fire again.

*September 29*

Difficulties in the third act of *Voyage*. Because I'm trying hard to express exactly what I imagine expressing. It's very difficult. I know very well what must be done and I can't do it.

More artillery fire. Wind continually from the south, clouds building.


*September 30*

Sylvie has had a very high fever since yesterday. I think it's simply a bad sore throat and quietly treat it as that. But with these polio epidemics I'm more anxious than usual. Aline is also sick, a boil, I believe, that requires a long, tiresome antibacterial cure, and I think, finally, the surgeon's scalpel. The other night, Uncle, dead drunk, fell the whole way down the pavilion stairs. He landed on his shoulder and lay there knocked out for over an hour, he says, under the vines. Since then, he can't undress himself or move his shoulder or his arm, which no one can look at because he keeps it hidden like a sacred object. As for me, my eyes ache and I have an annoying irritation in my left nostril. I'm stuck in the third scene of the third act. Nothing that I write satisfies me. I can see clearly what I want to do but I can't do it, can't create what I see and so powerfully imagine. What I want in this scene between Julio and Donna Fulvia is a very simple kind of pathos. The scene is very important, it's the big confrontation between J. and D.F. She's going to leave with the colonel and J. reproaches her for this coarseness. Given all she could have by herself, she has no need for the army or Napoleon. I want this to be in very simple, direct language and thus I'm aiming very high. I can see just what has to be done and can't manage to do it. And that's why I just forced myself to write this note, which is of no interest otherwise.

*October 1*

Sylvie is better, her fever has dropped. Aline continues with her cure. Uncle walks around with his arm hidden in a sling. He hasn't undressed by himself for eight days. My eyes continue to torment me. I'm still tangled up in my third scene although (or perhaps because) I never stop thinking about it day or night. Autumn is very beautiful. I've proposed to Mme. Bonnefoy that we lease the Criquet farm. The time I spend thinking about this third scene is interrupted by flashes of the work I'd like to devote to *Fragments* and *Grands chemins*.

*October 6*

Assuming that I eventually write a book, I couldn't care less if, a hundred years from now, some enthusiastic young scholar falls in love with it in a deadly boring high school class. Or even, if it's a masterpiece, if it contributes to the good of humanity, as it's pretentiously called. What matters to me is the lightning of making it (the book) and that's what I'd want the schoolboy to experience (or humanity for whom one must do good), so that he knows that one doesn't live in *historical reality*. The only historian I can read is Froissart, because he writes in *imaginary reality*. That's the reason to prefer Commines and really, leaping from one to the other, Lenin. What matters to me is writing the book, painting the fresco, composing *The Well-Tempered Clavier*, because I have my own "taste." I enjoy myself. The rest is for those whose "tastes" tend toward wanting all the credit. The art of making works and events say what they never said. And those are the very same ones constantly spouting the words "truths" and "true."

"What do you think of the news?"

"I don't read the newspapers and I don't listen to the radio." (If they were clever, they'd respond, "all the more reason.") Because what good does it do to tell them what I think.

Went out this evening at six o'clock to take the air after these four days of good work. Worn out, I got no farther than the café terrace. R. told me all about K.D.'s private affairs, fights with his wife who's sleeping with the doctor, and how he's supporting young B. At which point K.D. showed up and asked for a little tobacco. R. shook his hand. For five minutes they were "thick as thieves." No sooner had K.D. gone than R. says to me, in these very words, "I can't stand him. He's a liar, a fraud, it's a disgrace." In fact, K.D. is sleeping with young B., whom R. wants to sleep with. It's funny, but at the end of the day, what good can come from it? Five minutes later young B. showed up, K.D. hanging all over her. All that over drinks and sleeping arrangements. R. complaining to the waiter that his glass wasn't full enough: "If I were to claim my five centiliters." I didn't know one was entitled to five centiliters.

*October 7*

Today I went to the Margotte farm by bicycle. Left this morning, in the most gloriously fine weather, and returned at six o'clock at dusk through a very beautiful autumn shower that released all the season's scents. Salomé took me to see the Dragon farm – he calls it the grange – which borders ours and is up for sale. I haven't got a penny to buy it. But I agree that it would set us up nicely. Then I would own the beautiful moor with the tall oaks and the hill where I've dreamed of building a house. I can't bear the Manosque landscape. I think I'd find peace there. I only own part of the moor with the oaks, enough to build on, but in a limited way. Of course it would be magnificent if I could buy the Dragon farm. I'm imagining a workroom for myself due north with a window to the east. A mistake in our country of strong north winds, but so what, the wind will blow right against my window. I like a little bitter cold on my hands in the winter to heighten the comfort of the fire. But of course I haven't got the first penny for all that. Well, too bad, let's take a look anyway, the view doesn't cost anything. Or the dream. The Dragon farmer, his old wife, and his daughter (married, four children, four boys, she's thirty years old) (her husband lives in Berre, a factory worker no doubt. She's there to eat, she says; she says she has gained four kilos). These three characters plus a little boy of five, horribly dirty (enormous tears in the young woman's eyes, and black streaks running down her bare calves and thighs, which you could see beneath her half-open skirt), were sitting on the stones in the yard, stripping millet stalks with their bare hands. We made a grand tour of the estate, Salomé, the Dragon farmer, and me. It would complete the picture, no doubt about it. The more I look at it, the more I feel that it must be bought. That without it the Margotte farm is nothing (which isn't true). I can understand the desire to expand for someone whose whole game this is. It's enthralling. The Dragon farmer has no teeth, a blond mustache, an old white hat, a good little belly. Tall. Walks slowly. Keeps his land like a pig. We have a friendly dispute over three hundred square meters of moor that I've always considered mine. Then he shakes hands with us and quietly returns home. It's raining.

*October 10*

I believe that I'm deeply grateful for everything that forcefully cuts me off from the world. I'm coming to lose my friends with joy. Maybe I wouldn't be losing them if they were my friends. I responded to two young Bordeaux students regarding the article by Maurice Wullens on *Jeunes Forces*. Those two young men had written a very fair letter. And I answered Hélène L. on the same topic. I must explain myself here regarding that article, since I don't want to explain myself elsewhere.

*October 11*

This evening an anxious Élise came into my office and admitted to me that she was frightened. I asked her why and she hesitated. Finally she confessed that she was afraid for me because of the assassination attempts. I asked her why anyone would kill me. She said, "I don't know but the revolution has begun, I'm afraid for you. I would be less anxious if you hid. Go to our farms, go wherever you want. Don't worry about us. Don't stay here for us." I tried to make her understand that there's no reason for anyone to kill me.

Finished the third scene of the last act. Two more scenes. I can't wait to be done so I can start both *Fragments* and *Les Grands chemins* at the same time. But maybe I will finish *Deux cavaliers* first. But I'm in too much of a hurry finally to work on the big subject. I'll work on everything at the same time. And so the work must take the place for me of whatever is my subject. Did not finish clarifying my ideas on the Wullens case.


*October 12*


I can easily see Jean-Paul Sartre's *La Nausée* as a film. Because they're so vivid, Roquetin's silent schemes. Roquetin about to throw the stone. Roquetin who can't or doesn't dare fetch the paper. R. in front of his mirror. Life's dialogues and life's uneventfulness. But who for an actor? Why *Les Trois mousquetaires*?

Because there's action? There's action here as well. It would have to be a very long film. But if it gave us *La Nausée*, what a triumph! The Art of Cinema: this would be it. There's as much superimposition as you could want in this project, and "parallel lives," and dramatic reversals – these were timidly attempted elsewhere (Blanchar's film – dream of the jealous wife) – and beautiful symphonies in black and white or in color; so, grays and blues with ethereal golds for Rollebon, and the poetry of *The Threepenny Opera*. I can really see it. But how to do the whole book: not to cut anything, and get both the speeded up and slow motion. You're talking about one fantastic night!

*October 13*

This evening at six o'clock Aline came in to announce the visit of two gendarmes. I told her to show them in. They came to ask me for information on Lucien Jacques. It seems it's primarily a matter of supplies. Supplies? What, the black market? What a joke! Gentlemen, if you could see L.J., in five minutes you'd understand what a joke this is. But they insisted, and I insisted, he's poor, he doesn't give a damn about money, he's sick. He lives alone. He doesn't need anything. So then they came to the point. It seems he's supposed to be playing a major role in resupplying the resisters. Again, gentlemen, I laugh, that's an even bigger joke. Lucien never does anything political. Nothing political, stays away from all that. (Meanwhile I'm anxious to point out that Lucien Jacques is a Gentleman. You can't tell by what I've said that he's a poet and a painter. Nor if you saw his house, because he's poor. But he is a very important, very famous man. I have to keep insisting upon that, because being a poet, painter, poor – that's no good to a gendarme. They sit up and take notice when I say that he's very close to certain important figures.) Finally one of the gendarmes said to me, "And you, what do you do exactly?" "Well you see, I write, plays for the theater, for example, you know, right now, a play for the theater – " "Does it have anything to do with French?" "What???" "Yes," he said, "with French." (I thought maybe *Le Français* was a newspaper they imagined I contributed to and I was about to say no, and then I took a chance:) "You mean French composition?" (the gendarme lets out a sigh) "Yes, that's it! French composition." "Oh, well, yes," I say, "that's related to what I do, it's a little like French compositions." "Ah," says the gendarme, "because that's exactly what I have to do, a French composition." (I must have made a strange face!) After a pause I ask, "And what is this French composition?" "One often lies to his bosses, sometimes to his peers, never to his subordinates." (I am literally flabbergasted! I make him repeat it three times!!) I say to him, "Well that would certainly get me all muddled up." Nevertheless I try to explain to him, for example, that one lies to his bosses to avoid a responsibility; to his peers to seem superior (!), and never to his subordinates *because commanding them is sufficient*! That he understands well enough. But then I say to him, "Really, aren't those strange questions to be asked? Afterwards, won't they say to you: so, you lie to your superiors?" He's puzzled. I am too. "So you should begin," I say, "by telling them that one must never lie, in any case whatsoever. Because in my opinion," I say, "that whole thing is a trap." He laughs quietly and says, "That wouldn't surprise me."

At one point I wondered if they really were gendarmes. I wondered if they were going to draw their revolvers and start shooting. That lasted about ten seconds. Ten very chilly seconds. I continued to ramble on about French composition but the atmosphere had turned icy.

English radio announced this evening that Italy, through Marshall Badoglio, has declared war on Germany. Then followed an Italian voice that uttered, among other things, this astounding line: "Who could accuse us of having done an about-face?" (And they would like us to take all this seriously! No, it's simply homicidal madness, a kind of general running amok. If after all this, one still truly believes in a hereditary enemy (a different one each week), still trusts in a state's word and signature (Belgium,

France, Italy, and those that follow), still sees the *reason* for fighting between peoples, that would justify the most profound contempt for the whole human race. And we aren't at the end of these retractions.)

*October 14*

I'm more and more convinced that something new and amazing could be done in film with Sartre's *La Nausée*. By new, I mean a complete break with everything that already exists in film in terms of the poetic and fantastic. Especially the length of the film, surely not the present length (it would be meaningless at that length). Of course, it's not a question either of money, connections, or producers. It's only a question of art since the great preoccupation is the Art of Cinema. For example, when Roquentin goes to Café Mably that foggy day (p. 96) and then, after going to the library, he returns to the café to check on M. Fasquelle, despite his haste to return, unlike in the book, it must be represented without haste. Haste in film actors creates disorder. Or else use slow motion, make the actor run, and then slow down his actions until the moment he enters Café Mably and sees that the café is empty. (*La Nausée*) The sequences are really extraordinarily beautiful. I wonder why nobody has thought of it. For example, immediately following Café Mably (p. 105, 106, 107) the giant carapace that stirs the mud with its long claws, then the pervert, red with cold in his long cloak, who watches the little girl, and then suddenly the library, the reading room, Roquentin's hand at the table holding *La Chartreuse de Parme*, "refuge in the lucid Italy of Stendhal."

Finally, despite my repugnance for it (no desire at all to play investigator) I wrote Lucien a short note simply to inform him about the gendarmes's visit.

It's funny, that line from last evening: "Who could accuse us of having done an about-face?" It's funny and it's very Italian, Stendhal's Italian. The gentleman who puts on Louis XV heels to get his ass kicked. Fine, without words. With words, disgusting. And the poor bastards keep letting themselves be killed, because they aren't getting themselves killed anymore, they're letting themselves be killed.

*October 17*

Into my little office today, battered with rain and clouds, came G.M.R. to tell me about her marriage. It's in two weeks. She's nineteen years old, strong, with a little mustache, dark, well built, very healthy and so sensual that one sees her as though in an American film, assailed with a sensuality that will be her undoing. She's marrying a cold, pale creature, a chemical engineer for Rhône Aspirin. She says she's fed up with the preliminaries for the wedding. She'd like to be married to a Strauss waltz played on the organ and with a bouquet of sunflowers in her hands. "Why not?" she asks me. Of course, I nod. Her plans for their life are staggering. Unhappy chemist, how will he fulfill his vows to the gods of chemistry? I give her some fatherly advice and she leaves very determined to be the whale of adultery. I imagine (and it's obvious) what monstrous dreams she has. This will take place in two weeks under the most bourgeois auspices imaginable.

*October 20*

This evening I returned from Margotte by bicycle. Returned by the Villeneuve road that I didn't know. Too tired to write down everything I worked out along the way. Before *Fragments*, I have to write *Deux cavaliers*. Saw how I can reconstruct it with what exists. The plateau leaving Forcalquier toward Villeneuve is very beautiful, almost transforming. A wide open view of the Alps. To see it again someday in the great winter wind with clouds.

Streams of light. A new view of the Saint-Maime side. The village of Dauphin like a king's crown on playing cards. Also thought about *Fragments*, that its construction seems right to me and accommodates beautiful things.

*October 21*

Returning to *Deux cavaliers*. Poetic composition falling outside the usual rules of composition. The Jasons' story, then Ariane's conversations about the town (which are written but without any of the women's conversations clearly focused on the savagery and brutality of that town), then Marceau's dream. To give clarity to the composition, and fierceness. To leave only the essential, to center the whole story around its strength. But above all, a great variety of points of view in the composition. A single description of the country (very important) when Marceau dies. The end must be a powerful explosion that self-destructs. Ariane remained standing. She didn't act like an old woman. She straightened up, took a deep breath, and waved her arms like an athlete. She speaks (and immediately a description of the town begins).

In the fights, not to trust comparisons, take out the marriage of the cadet and the woman. Unnecessary tenderness. Clean it up.

Course of events. Arrival of "American civilization" in a France divided and without desire for grandeur. Abundance, redundant speeches, Capuan delights, all right here. A few weeks of personal vendettas; everything is settled. All the hundred-year-old quarrels between neighbors, all the small-time Capulets and Montaigus, Saint Bartholomew's Day for the envious and the ruined. Bouvard and Pécuchet of the machine gun. A mix of *Ubu roi*, radical-socialist agricultural shows, and the slaughterhouse. Then it'll go to the polls where the Communist party will take over legally.

"The powers (sublime with regard to elections) of the ventriloquist…"

H. de Balzac (*Le Député d'Arcis*)

We are headed toward the victory and reign of the ventriloquist. "The price of cotton depended upon the triumph or defeat of Emperor Napoleon, about whom his adversaries, the English generals, said in Spain: "The city is taken, let the idiots advance." (H. de Balzac, *Le Député d'Arcis*) With France taken, we can let the idiots advance. The spirit would remain. Germany after 1815. But the Cossacks were only bogeymen. Alexander was beautiful as the day. Stalin doesn't bother with beauty salons.

While I was writing, the dull rumbling of a big bomb in the

distance, then anti-aircraft defense overhead. I opened the window. At that moment Charles knocked on my door. "You hear the bombing?" "I opened the window," I say. We try to guess the direction. Maybe Avignon. But the wind is from the south so my guess would be Marseille instead. We'll find out tomorrow. Charles says, "The war's getting closer."

*October 22*

This morning, the newspaper had nothing about bombing in neighboring areas. And we can still hear muffled blasts in the distance. No doubt these are defense exercises. But last evening, last night, all that dark rumbling was truly epic. The wind has been from the south for several days. Rarely have I seen clouds as beautiful as the ones now rising. A moment ago, the east was masked by an enormous black band and the light came from the west in three long straw-colored streaks that reversed all the shadows. Then as the wind shifted everything went back to normal.

*October 23*

At eight o'clock this morning Mme. Seguin came to let me know that Meyerowitz has been arrested and is headed for the Mées concentration camp. Doing what I can to help him. At noon C. came to see me with the same news and to try to coordinate efforts. He'll go to the bishop's office (M. has a strong letter of support from the nuncio), I'll go to the police, and Ch., who was alerted in Marseille by telegram, will see the prefecture.

Feeling a great need to be done with *Voyage*. Finished scene IV today; I'm on the last scene. I can't wait to be less strapped for money. For organized solitude. But *Voyage* is made up of small drops and I need a project that draws more generously from what I really am, that can be a very powerful siphon. In this regard, taking up *Cavaliers* again will help me. To acquire a style again, which is also a life style. I remember a time when I spent many hours at a stretch at my desk. Now I go there to jot down two or three good lines between hours spent on the divan. I don't feel like I'm working but like I'm trying to. To regain that healthy abundance of work as with *Batailles dans la montagne* or *Que ma joie*, and to make a work of art without thinking about anything else.

*October 24*

A.F. showed me an article in *Jeunes Forces de France* on *Les Vrais richesses* reproaching me for my bank account and my checkbook. What a joke. First of all it's hard to relate a checkbook to a book, but more to the point, there would have to be a real checkbook. The French consider themselves rich if they have 50,000 francs. I don't have that kind of money. I don't have 50,000 francs, free and at my disposal. I work precisely to make a living. I have nine people to feed, my two farms are tiny and they cost rather than make me money. I'm not complaining about that. I have to solicit my publishers three or four times a year and right now I have exactly 20,000 francs in my Crédit Lyonnais account (that's easy to verify) and I owe 60,000 to the tax collector and 32,000 to the builder who fixed up the apartments at Margotte, and I've asked Hamonic at Grasset for an advance of 50,000 francs. So the legend is established. But all this leaves me perfectly indifferent and I'm quietly explaining it to myself just to take stock.

On the subject of M. Wullens's article, I've decided that it would be cowardly to offer any explanation. I can say that I've thought about it for a long time now and in the end I don't have anything to say.

*October 26*

Spent the last two days getting Meyerowitz out of the Mées camp, foreign workers camp no. 702. Monday I went to Mées. It was raining so hard that M. phoned to tell me to put it off until Tuesday. But I had already left and Élise took the call. It was pouring at the Peyruis station where I got off and through the rain I saw M. arriving who said, "The captain has sent a car for you." It's three kilometers from Peyruis to Mées. We climbed into a farm truck also carrying two gendarmes from Nice accompanying a Jew. We drove with all three of them through the downpour. We arrived sopping wet. The camp, the office, the captain. Like Hurluret, but what humanity! Over the course of the day, he told me that he had to save France, that he was a radical socialist, that, above all, he was a patriot, that he had been a tie salesman, that he was a mathematician, that he had saved Italian officers, that he had survived 1940, that he had stashed 250,000 francs for his company in his flannel binder, that he had seen a flag burned, that everything was going to work out for M. His wife appeared at noon, drank wine with us. Must be the company's backbone. Makes care packages for the prisoners of war, enlivens the place, plays mother for the group, but I'm editing our conversations, and she sent a few guys she didn't like to the factory, and she has such light blue eyes, and a smile on her pretty, tired, old-looking face. Hurluret kissed the hollow of her elbow and arm in the café. I did the honors. Beside me, M., scared and obsequious, played the fool nevertheless. Finally at four o'clock I bought M.: twelve hundred francs a year in payments of a hundred francs a month, and the camp released him to me as a farm worker at Margotte, so in Forcalquier. M. is going to live in Forcalquier. And I returned through the same rain, a packed train, an hour late, and only green beans to eat when I got home, so-called *green*: hard, stringy, inedible. In a silent rage. A terrible effort the entire day to be nice. Left by bike for Forcalquier yesterday to sort out M.'s situation. Returned in the evening dead tired. Received four letters.

At the Peyruis station that evening, M., who had repeated incessantly all day, "I'm running the greatest risks," did not stop repeating, "I've run the greatest risks." I hope that in Forcalquier he'll find a piano and a place to live and can work peacefully, but the captain said to him, "be retiring as a violet."

I can't tell if M. really considers us friends, or even likes me. And my lack of confidence no doubt makes me treat him very unjustly. It's not out of spite but for fear of being duped. I'm hard to understand until one learns that I'm very shy and all my kindnesses don't come naturally and cost me dearly. I only feel comfortable alone or with very, very simple people: Barbara, my cleaning woman, Charles. I'm not even at ease with Salomé, as simple as he is, but that's because I do him too many favors. I gave him a team of work horses, a harvester, a trotter, a cow, had the sheds rebuilt, gave him an electric pump, a shredder (with which he earns 2,000 francs a week by his own admission), I gave him a radio worth 6,000 francs, and I'm sure I'm forgetting to include in this list a good third of what I've given him. This prevents me from being at ease with him. I was never comfortable with Lucien Jacques. I liked him and that feeling troubled me considerably.

My shyness, which I'm constantly suppressing, robs me of all naturalness and simplicity. And being so patient, so stubborn, so pigheaded about following through with my plans, so faithful to my family ties, I have neither patience nor fidelity for "the ordinary" and I withdraw as soon as I'm hurt. And that's immediately. And that's why I'm unsociable. I have a horrible disgust for being duped. I can't excuse it.

I went down to find something to eat (for lunch there was stuffed eggplant which I don't like); Mme. Ernst was in the dooryard with Charles who was chopping wood. "Bad news," she said, "I have to have an operation. Something wrong with my stomach, it's going to be expensive." I asked how much. Five thousand francs. I told her to come see me Saturday. I would really love to get an answer from Grasset about the advance of 50,000 francs that I asked for. They just published new editions of *Naissance* and *Que ma joie*. They should be able to, it seems to me.

At four o'clock a visit from Pierre Sauvageot. Came to talk to me about the natural cultivation of wheat. Wheat sown grain by grain, spaced, mounded and hoed. Experiments with an extraordinary range of Egyptian wheats. He spoke at length, improvising a magnificent apocalypse for races fed on products grown with chemical fertilizers. It was all very beautiful. I'm going to venture reproducing it. This interests me with regard to *Grands chemins*. I told him that. He gave me some documents. I'm noting it here so there's a record somewhere that he provided me with these documents, in case I use them in some dramatic fashion, that I personally know nothing about the matter, and that all credit should go to him, not me. But there's no question that if I can make this apocalypse occur in *Les Grands chemins* I will broaden the scope of the novel significantly.

Which is not to forget that the goal of the work on *Fragments* and *Les Grands chemins* is to offer an embryonic Renaissance poetics. The elements of the Renaissance. Balzac. *Le Député d'Arcis*, I'm thinking of Stendhal's *Lucien Leuwen*. It's like that; although neither one is finished. I can imagine an end to *Député* that could become very Stendhalian by following the line pursued so far. *Les*

*Chouans*, another Stendhalian book, but with Stendhal, the love scenes between Marie de Verneuil and the Gars in the coach and the inn would have been an immense, sharp-edged, dazzling diamond. Balzac's a bit soft. And nevertheless the whole book has the sheen and sometimes the iridescence of *Chartreuse de Parme*. All of that very much beyond the Dickens that I'm in the process of reading this evening (*Nicholas Nickleby*) where the story doesn't escape "Punch": caricature, sentimentality. It's very engaging, despite some long passages that seem to drag on, but it remains a sketch, witty, exceptionally well constructed, but constructed. The two French works have more to them, they're richer, not in abundance but in grandeur and depths. Density. They can't be exhausted so quickly. It seems as though they'd sustain you through long months in prison.

Aline is excited about the Egyptian wheat.

*October 27*

MADAME BARE: That man over there (Thios, that is Théophile), you can't imagine how dirty he is. His hands are like feet!
MADAME BARE: (recipe for making goat cheese): You let your milk sit all night. The next day you strain out the flies.

A little gem from Montagne de Lure.

Give me victory over those I love and over those I hate.

Astounding! My intervention to save Meyerowitz has stirred up the whole Jewish hive in Manosque. Of course M. is Jewish, absolutely, although he hides it, although he's Catholic (is that why?), Jewish mouth, nose, heart, and soul, but apparently all the Jews collaborated in the anonymous denunciation that sent him to Mées. They worked with the police chief who belongs to the Francist Movement. That is to say, they denounced M. to the chief. One can get lost in the complexities here, clever, under-handed, an element of spitefulness. So, great fool that I am, I go to Mées and I get M. out of there without even wondering whether or not he's Jewish, knowing only that he's in trouble, and all that seems to have backfired on me. I can't believe my bad luck. Each time I turn immediately and instinctively toward something that seems to me simply human, it looks like I'm doing something stupid. Mean spiritedly, M. (on his way from Mées) told me little annoying things about Mme. Ernst this morning. It made me so sick that he saw it in my face. "Maybe I was wrong to tell you this," he said. I assured him that I never withhold my help, no matter what I think of the one I'm helping (M. for example about whom I have no illusions), but everything he said seems true and Mme. Ernst suddenly seems unjust to me. Because for over three years, I've continually given her *more than I promised her*: money (out of my own pocket), practical help with those in power (she remains here because I welcomed her with out-stretched arms, no papers, no identity card, nothing), spiritual help (having her translate *Triompe de la vie* into German – listening carefully to her personal plans, encouraging her – welcoming her regularly to my home).

*October 28*

*Les Chouans* (Balzac). There's something like a present-day atmosphere. The past and future face-to-face, the rubble, the ambushes, the dangers of the road, a taste for intrigue, a lack of nobility, the seductiveness of revolutionary youth (suddenly I realize that's what Communism is lacking: youth. A young Communist is no longer young, neither in physical appearance or soul. They've replaced enthusiasm with calculation and intel-lect. Communist revolutionaries are all old in mind and body, and moreover, the staunchest of them are old professors, old teachers, old students). Impossible for Balzac to speak of them as he speaks of Merle and Gérard in the Gars's castle (Pléiade, p. 904): "he seemed to have one of those truly Republican spirits which, in the days of which we write, crowded the French armies, and gave them, by means of these nobly humble devotions…" So here, in a word, lies another explanation: present-day devotions are humble but not noble. The Republican ideal requires nobility. The Communist ideal requires nothing but success. Hence its quick renunciation of nobility. The Republic is very beautiful once again under the Empire.

Earlier on that same page: "…those lines which gave, in those days, an expression of great candor and nobleness to young heads." I'm thinking of Communist revolutionaries. They have the cold, wrinkled heads of mathematicians, bitter, wasted. The revolution of M. Brauman, of Jean Perrin.

One could argue that this hardly matters, but where is there beauty to be found in the Communist revolution and a Communist state?

And we know very well that it matters! And Aragon, and Malraux, and my dear old Guéhenno? (Reread in Lenin the whole *Iskra* period and see what connections there are.)

*The Adventures of David Balfour* by Stevenson. The extraordinary pursuit from chapter 20 to chapter 31. Extremely sensitive musical composition. The reality of night, cold, water, and dread. But it's better and more sensitive in *Les Chouans* when Marie de Verneuil, Francine, and Galope-Chopine go to the Gars's ball (Pléiade, p. 971–977), there's true composition, not just in length but in sensitive depths. With the description of Fougères (p. 928–932) an immense resonant landscape is established that reverberates for a long time. (The Fougères attack, p. 915–955, is as astonishing as Waterloo in *La Chartreuse*.) Stendhal might have given *richness* to Marie's passion, but he would have neglected the orchestra. The basses, violins, and violas have to play their parts, but the horns must ring out as well. And if somewhere, at the precise moment, a drum beats, maybe that will make the dull symphony burst forth in the blaze of some emotion from the gut or "pit of the stomach." Then, what iridescence (rainbow)! Skipping stones in water. Nothing of all that holds true for Stevenson. With the art of Balzac and Stendhal, we have an essentially French art. Stevenson addresses the epidermis. Dickens as well, with naive attempts to go deeper in a crude way. The two French writers are *rogues*.

*Les Chouans* (Pléiade, p. 975). A sentence sounding very much like the Cervantes of *Don Quixote:* "Hardly had they gone a few miles through those woods than they heard in the distance the vague murmur of voices and the sound of a bell…" – The scene is set with a single stroke and the mystery unfolds. We are going to "eat the flute and drink the cymbal." But Balzac continues: "… a bell whose silvery tones did not have the monotony that the movements of cattle imprint upon them." And it's bad

Balzac. "Imprint" especially is unbearable, vulgar, false, and wrong. Stendhal wouldn't have used "imprint." But then Stendhal wouldn't have had that Cervantian sentence.

Often the sentence that has just swelled, expanded and sparkled in the light, bursts and resolves into a tiny drop of soapy water. We are not only vexed (this might be nothing, but it might be something), but also troubled as what we were looking at disappears. Hence, some uncertainty at times, increased by the many mistakes in word choice. It's like if you water down alcohol. It loses its potency.

Sylvie arrived home from school very overexcited: she saw leaflets falling! This is the first time, she points out as an excuse. No one heard the least sound of engines. Imagine the surprise of a bombing from that height.

*Les Chouans*. Description of the waltz danced by Marie de Verneuil and the Gars (Pléiade, p. 1001), example of description of a thing totally unknown by the author and very foreign to his nature. Wrong words (*roula*) and all lackluster. Some emotion remains because it's Balzac and because it's moving to know that Balzac never waltzed with a woman in love and passionately loved. No divination. It's here that Stendhal (even having never waltzed) might have worked wonders. He might have made of it a *description of Fougères*.

Just before the description of the waltz, moreover, and undoubtedly at the moment when Balzac, well underway, sensed that he was about to describe something unknown, there's this ghastly image, ugly and above all false: "kept the secret of her thoughts as the sea swallows those of the criminal who casts a weighted body into its depths." We get lost in the comparison between Marie's beautiful head and the sea, between "thoughts" (*pensées*) and "weighted" (*pesant*) body. "Those of," which replaces "secret," is so questionable that we don't know right away what it's replacing and we have to reread the whole thing, emphasizing "those of," to understand the construction. Here is the fear of the writer who, in a moment, is about to fall into the unknown and is already stumbling. He is in the process of trying to save beauty and he writes rubbish. We would need to know why, at that moment, Balzac thought of comparing Marie's thoughts to the "product of a crime." Because once he wrote the word "sea," he could have, and normally he would have, thought of fish, and then there's only one mistake: face and sea (especially a face described so: "unfathomable gentleness of her eyes," "the demure smile on her lips" etc., is not *comparable* to the sea). Furthermore, there is no crime to hide here; he says so himself, she has nothing to conceal but her flattery and vanity. So, why the devil this "weighted body"? It's Balzac who interests me here. Cave of bats.

*October 29*

An ambiguous letter from Hamonic on the 50,000 francs that I asked for. He's not sending it. Grasset will have to write to me, it seems. I'm going ahead and writing to him first. Since 1929, I've never asked for a single penny in advance. My credit has always been good with my publisher. To an extreme, and that's rare, I think. And this time, it's not even an actual advance, simply an advance on the 160,000 francs that they'll owe me in two months, after the deluxe edition of *Pan* and *Que ma joie demeure* comes out. Instead of making things simple, they deliberate. It seems like I'm asking them for charity or a huge favor. A letter to Grasset, not angry but firm. Because what good does it do to get angry.

*Les Chouans* – Toward the end, there is no more debate, nothing more to see, we are swept along, no wrong word choices, no "imprint," nothing. There's only the Gars, Marie, the Chouans climbing the precipice, the Bleus' silent march in the fog. Death that thunders, about to explode into lightning. Only Corentin, whose dishonor I don't entirely see. At that point, one excuses all baseness. We know they're going to die. A magnificent book that never lags, to be read all in one sitting. Many wonderful passages, descriptions of the country and battles. The death of Galope-Chopine, the ball, the mass in the forest. Marie and

Francine walking to the ball. Description of Fougères. Lacks the sparkling diamond heart that Stendhal would have given the love between Marie and the Gars. That's the weak part. Or at least we know that it's been done better. As for the rest of it, no one has ever done it better.

Strange, too, how Garganoff is behaving. We've signed a contract for my plays. Fine. Moreover, according to the contract he gets the plays for free and he gets half the royalties, under the pretext that he'll be in charge of them. Fine. He's had *La Femme du boulanger* for over a year and he hasn't staged it. I'm doing that. I found him, for free, a large theater in Paris, a smart director (Cocéa) who'll cover all the costs, he'll get half the royalties, for nothing, and still he writes me an insolent letter because I signed what? A little paper from the Société des Auteurs by which I agree to give the play to Cocéa and Cocéa agrees to take it from me, period, that's it. He calls this a contract and he claims that the only reason he's not suing me is because he's a good soul. What wrong have I done him? On the contrary: rereading the contract carefully, I get nothing out of doing plays. On that point (and as a kindness) I'm doing one more (*Le Voyage*) and I'm giving it to Cocéa as well. He doesn't have to do a thing and he gets half the royalties without having paid *a single penny* to buy the play, or to produce it, or to advertise it, nothing. I'm not complaining about the contract, I signed it. I'm complaining about his insolence. And this is my friend! Actually I'm not complaining. I'm writing it down. It's a joke.

*October 31*

I just this moment finished the third act of *Voyage*. But Aline has a sore throat, Sylvie is coughing, and I just applied a poultice, and Élise just went to lie down saying, "I'm not sick but I'll feel better lying down." And she is sick.

*November 2*

Aline has a wicked sore throat that hasn't responded to three days of painting it. We're out of cotton, we're out of iodine; finally, today, it seems better. Élise has been in bed for three days and isn't completely over some vague digestive trouble. Sylvie feels better and is doing her homework. Began to reread the *Aeneid* to compare against the 200 best pages of the Corrêa edition. I don't find in the translation published by Belles Lettres the vivid emotion of the Hinstin translation published by Lemerre that I read in the orchards on Sundays in spring in my youth. But the secret must lie in the orchard, Sunday, spring, and youth (to be verified, even so).

It's raining a Chinese rain. Dark figures of women are slowly climbing the small hill under my window, sheltered by big umbrellas. The whole country streaked with white lines. The firs hunched over in their great coats. It's beginning to get cold in my house. Cleaned my stove with Charles and installed a new heater in the big chimney that doesn't draw well. The stove with its flues draws, but too much, and roars, which I hate. Scared stiff of fire. Why? Atavism? That fire my father often talked about, in which his father lost all he had and the wages of the workers at the Zola building site near Aix. My father told me that was the first time he saw the moon. He was nine years old, but brought up the hard way, he was in bed every evening by six o'clock. That night he was snatched in his nightshirt from the blazing house and on his mother's knees, from the meadow, he saw the moon. That was more striking to him than the fire in which two men burned to death. Even so, he must have been afraid and must have passed that on to me. I have never witnessed any fires. Out of fear, I'm insured and double insured. I have a physical terror of a roaring stove. Reinstalled in the mantel of the large fireplace, my stove roars terribly. I made use of fire in *Colline*. I described it with delight, I remember, one winter morning when my room was so cold that my fingers froze. Élise begged me to make a fire.

I wouldn't have done that for all the money in the world. I would have sooner stopped writing. That was in the big black house on Grand Rue. In my father's old workshop where we'd added a kitchen after he died, and where we were all living, Élise, my mother, Uncle, and me. Aline had just been born.

I just reread some passages from the Hinstin translation. It's not quite as well translated as the André Bellessort that I'm working through. It's just as I thought, a matter of youth and enthusiasm. A little while ago, Henri (Fluchère) came to see me, very good, fine, calm, peaceful, a good friend, faithful and just. I'm the bad character here, thin-skinned, arrogant, proud, and lacking the most basic generosity. Fluchère talked to me about the work he's doing on Shakespeare and Elizabethan theater. Very coherent, accurate views on the relationship between Machiavelli and Seneca. It's true that in each play there's a Machiavelli and that, after brandishing increasingly bloody hearts on the points of daggers, the only recourse left is Seneca's stoicism (which I don't possess). For my part, it's been more than six months since I read *The Prince*, joyfully and fruitfully.

The small clandestine journal *Les Lettres françaises* that I receive provides some information on the book A. Malraux has been working on for the last three years. One certainly can't judge from the excerpts in this summary, which aren't given much space. But if the article's accurate, Malraux would be no more than a kind of Maurice d'Esparbès for the lower class.

All this sucking up to the Russians, is it sincere? Doesn't he overdo it a bit? It all seems compelled by money, or the desire for an eminent position afterwards, or having succumbed to some propaganda. There's too much of it. I get the impression that those who are offended by the poetics of Pilniak (and who are remarkably intelligent) will also be offended by this poetics of intelligence. Odds are that a strong victorious Communist party would kick out M. André Malraux. Lesson: too much fawning blurs our vision, whether from the simple perspective of art or even the opposite perspective of service to a party. What I'm going to copy below is insufferable, indefensible, badly conceived, and badly constructed.

"*The troops had received orders to advance toward the second enemy lines*" (I'm copying from *Les Lettres* but what I'm highlighting is from Malraux). Doctor Hoffmann is growing impatient. Strange men in shirtsleeves come out of the trench, but "*the wave of assault did not head toward the Russians, it came back*." It's impossible to summarize this part of the work here. Nevertheless it constitutes the essential lesson. It is the eruption of indignation, the explosion of revolt, the impassable limit of the inhuman. To the humiliation of action, to the humiliation of thought, to the humiliation of courage, is supposedly added the humiliation of human brotherhood in the face of death, the humiliation of a kind of vague love of life, as if in the presence of helpless suffering, anger and shame did not suddenly arise." (Parenthesis: all of that except the italicized lines are the journal speaking.) "*The spirit of evil here was even stronger than death, so strong that it was necessary to find a Russian who hadn't been killed, any Russian at all, to drape him over his shoulders and save him.*" (Another parenthesis – this is from Malraux.) This is what I call sucking up because why a Russian!? In the passage that line comes from, it's supposedly a matter of decent German soldiers who attacked with gas and who are saving the gassed Russians. But, and this isn't logical, but these lines make me think of the time in my childhood when it was the poor Chinese children who had to be saved. The Germans didn't attack with gas, as far as I know, and if tomorrow it was the Russians who attacked with gas, would M. Malraux applaud them, repeating his own words: "*The wave of assault did not head toward the Germans, it came back*" and "*…it was necessary to find a German who hadn't been killed, any German at all, to drape him over his shoulders and save him.*" I know very well what M. Malraux will say: No, my Russians are the future, your Germans are the past, nothing at all, pigs, Nazis, there's no possible comparison, Russians are saved, yes, indignation, humiliation, anger, shame, in short, everything the journal says, but that's because Russians are attacked (who barely three years ago were in accord with the Germans about carving up Poland together). The humiliation of human brotherhood in the face of death, as they say above, does it apply in both cases or only, as at the circus, in my favor? I don't find anything great in these little expressions of popular propaganda. Bad Epinal imagery. Malraux, do you think the Russians, any more than the Germans, are truly capable of revolt in honor of the love of life, as you say, in the presence of helpless suffering, as you say? Do you think, Malraux, that anger and shame will rise up somewhere, anywhere, look, that it'll rise up in you yourself, for example, in the face of all the helpless suffering that, as victor, you'll inflict with as much cruelty and injustice as the Germans are doing now? *Les Lettres françaises* journal (which must be Communist) says that this passage constitutes the essential lesson, but I maintain that if the Germans or the Russians attacked with gas tomorrow, there would be no revolt, no shame, no anger, no humiliation of a vague love of life. Everything would happen *as usual*, that's how it is, horrible, and no one would be outraged. I don't think the Germans are a chosen race, but more importantly I don't think the Russians are. Neither one nor the other. God isn't French, but neither is he a foreigner.

And the paragraph continues: "And Vincent Berger (that's the hero) who, swept up in this chaos, also dragged a dead Russian onto his back and is attempting pathetically to save a corpse, *watched wide-eyed, relieved, as the onslaught of pity came crashing toward the ambulances.*"

It used to be a daily coin donated to the church to save Chinese children, now it seems to be all our blood donated to the church of M. Malraux and Co. to save the "good Russians." There's something deadly comic in this, that's all.

Another comic matter, this one personal, stems from the discrepancy between my actual financial situation and the myth circulating on this subject. X. told me this again yesterday in Marseille, I'm considered very rich. It infuriates the "pure youth" that I have a checkbook. It's true, I do have one. Right now I have a grand total of 32,000 francs in my Crédit Lyonnais account. Salomé is coming to ask me for 2,500 francs to buy casks for my wine. I owe Porporat 37,000 francs for work at Margotte. Mme. Ernst enters the hospital Monday and is counting on me to pay for her operation (6,000?). Salomé wants to borrow 50,000 from me to buy a little horse at the fair in Gap. I'm going to have to turn him down. But even so, I don't have enough to pay Porporat and the taxes I still owe, 80,000. I owe 80 + 37 + 6 = 123,000 and I have 30,000. No response from Grasset about the 50,000 I asked for. I have never had money. What surprises them is that it doesn't bother me. Well, not very much. What does bother me is not being able to lend Salomé 50,000. No. Everything about it bothers me. And what a waste of time thinking about it!

Everything is working out. At noon the 50,000 arrived from Grasset with a nice letter. What's more, they only had to advance me 35,000. I had credit for 15,000 in my account. A nice simple letter sending me the money and saying a letter would follow from Grasset, which I haven't received yet. Mother Ernst will be able to have her operation.

Wednesday, Thursday, Friday in Marseille. Hôtel de Paris. They're nice. The hotel clerk was sucking up a little, I don't remember regarding what (filling out my guest card no doubt), "famous writer," he said, "known throughout the world," he added. He was an old man, you couldn't be angry with him, that was annoying. The next minute, I was thanking him stupidly, awkwardly, like I would give a coin to a beggar. I wanted to tell him to get lost. Three days of divine joys. Life gives me loads of joys. And I am more and more capable of savoring them, of enjoying them fully. The quality of what I'm given is so magical that it's as though I'm living in an enchanted city. Nothing exists beyond my joy. It's the essential fabric. I move through the streets like an underwater diver. Restaurant, faces, it's all tulle (like Cocéa's forest). It's all scenery, though not ugly because the rest is so beautiful, so *golden*, so fantastically real that it banishes the ordinary in life to extraordinarily remote distances. The impression that we leave our mark in the street. A beautiful mark, the mark of joy in sadness, maybe even purity (that must be seen), well, certainly unusual. They stand there opened mouth, sometimes literally. The completely appalling humanity of the city. Men and women with fish heads, pig heads (many of these), snake heads (without chins), parrot heads (the women), dog heads, cat heads, tomato heads, empty heads as well, many of them, the majority. Apollos among them as well, but you can tell immediately they have the hearts of hollow radishes just seeing what care they take that the crease in their trousers doesn't get rumpled. And what spastic jerking all the bones in their skeletons have to endure so that their jackets remain impeccable as they walk. And their eyes! If they are a beautiful color (which happens, velvet black), they are no less cold. If not, they are the ugliest part of the whole city, the eyes of the Apollos, not diabolical, no, not even when they're beautiful, that's what makes them terrible, absolutely cut off from all good or evil gods, that's the color of their eyes. There are also Venuses, and here it's simply a matter of their asses, not even clean, that's for sure. Night is falling. A horrible sensation. To be far away. Happily. No different from being in the hills with the red leaves right now and the wonderful yellow-gold of the medlar trees. When we were alone in the phantasmagoria of the solitary olive orchards. Always the same and it's beautiful. Ugliness will not enter, cannot even seep in. Watertight. Completely.

*November 7*

First day of a brisk mistral in a long time. Great frenzy of light and cold. Sky sparkling from one edge to the other. The hills dazzlingly bright. Red leaves in droves. Rumbling, drums. Frantic gestures of trees that lash the flocks of leaves with their black whips.

The beginning of the New Middle Ages, as announced in the first pages of *Chute de Constantinople*. Robberies (the armed robbery of the tobacco shop in Simiane can hardly pass for a patriotic act of war), large companies occupying the high hills and even T.S. Eliot's *Murder in the Cathedral*. The priest in La Fontaine de Vaucluse was killed. The newspaper report could have been for the ecclesiastical murders of the tenth to thirteenth centuries: "Two shots were fired that wounded the unfortunate priest. Retreating, Father Ameilh took refuge in a side chapel, then at the foot of the high alter. His assailants pursued him mercilessly and shot many more times to finish him off." This article from 1943 ends with a paragraph on the desecrated church that will be closed and off-limits until it can be reconsecrated. The incidents created by gangs of robbers and murderers will necessitate strongholds, communities withdrawing into themselves, and probably a kind of knighthood, and maybe the white gatherings that I spoke of in *Chute*. Round Table. In Marseille, Z. told me that during his stay in Nyons a Gaullist rally was announced right out in the open. Roads, streets, and alleys guarded by the gendarmes. The curiosity of people who came to watch, pretending they hadn't; counter-demonstrations by the Youth camps who marched past singing *La Marseillaise*. Atmosphere of unrest and insecurity. All that, if the Communists looked at it with their eyes open, goes beyond the revolutionary stage. It's already post-revolution (post aborted revolution), with outbreaks of fighting or attempts of fighting amidst widespread insecurity. There are no mystical ferment. For the moment at least. The Middles Ages without faith, without lords, without fortified castles, without chivalry, without Christianity (or whatever might replace it – because Communism will not replace it because it is so crudely material, because it hasn't realized that the spirit is also matter, and what matter!). In any case, this is going to continue, to grow and expand, to increasingly turn away from all that might have been noble about it at the start; it's going to devolve into murder pure and simple, hotfooted armed robberies of isolated farms, busses, cars, forming gangs like Cartouche and Mandrin. Good material for novelists.

I'm gradually realizing that the place where I live (my office) is wonderful. Not in the way that Lucien might find wonderful maybe, not Côte d'Azur or Saint-Paul or the Contadour. Nothing sensational. But right, and radiant with light. I was reading on my divan and I looked at my south window out of which, in full sun scoured clean by the mistral, swayed the shining cypress and I had to come note down my contentment. It's true that it's a Greek day outside. One of those icy, brilliant Sundays on which, when I was young, I would go on magnificent personal odysseys in the olive orchards, which have since become my Armida's gardens.

Having no inner resources, that's the curse of men who live in cities (Marseille), where those who have them lose them or leave. Territories without beauty.

Today, the ceaseless rush of violent wind around my high room. The sound of wind battering my north wall. Outside it's pure diamond. Unbearable brilliance of an earth without form or color. All that exists open to the heart is a naked gray sky that captures all the light. The earth is nearly black.

In Marseille, I saw a movie in color. *La Ville dorée*. A mediocre film except for the choice of faces (almost as right as in American movies). Color, although used discretely and magnificently for the first time, remains irrelevant to life. But precisely in this irrelevance, what possibilities for poetry! In the falseness that is color, what potential for latent poetic powers. I was speaking recently of *La Nausée*. What I mean about the poetry of color can be expressed more clearly in relation to this film project. It's not in a film's exterior – flesh of horses, ponds, flowers, skies, clouds, skin tones of faces, the beautiful green eyes of the heroine – that color must function, but in the poetry. Sartre's *La Nausée* in color. That's where we could really see what color can do. I think that as soon as films in color become the rule, the black and white film will disappear as the silent film has. Only here we are headed toward extraordinary vulgarities. Colors are going to be slapped on wildly, none of the plays you can discover with a new keyboard scale. If I were allowed – please heaven – to be able to freely – I say freely – film *Le Chant du monde*, and if it were to be in color, I would love to try to use those new tones not to make the grass green – although it would be green – but to make a crimson or ochre or grayish pink enter suddenly into the drama as Lady Macbeth enters or the witches or Ariel! Of course it would all be in color, but suddenly a dramatic color would enter – maybe a lowly gray – and the gray would play – *that's the essential thing, would have to play* – the same role as an action, word, or music. *Ville dorée*, a trite story, and nevertheless the red dress and crown of wheat and the festive golds in the costume of the servant girl who is getting engaged to the master; when the servant girl follows behind her dark master like a caged bear, at the moment when first the girl appears, and then disappears, and the whole party leaves for the pond to stop her from drowning herself. A moment of very high drama. Very brief but very high.

*November 8*

A.F. who came to see me this morning told me a funny little story that made me roar with laughter. It was in the Marseille station. The train for Saint-Raphaël packed to the gills by the porters, the steps crowded with passengers holding on. On the platform a dazed German soldier under a tremendous load of bags; he had no idea where to board, where to find a spot. He looked around, he was the last one on the platform, they were only waiting for him to blow the whistle for departure. Then one of the crew went up to him and said to him in patois, "Alors, *ounclé, parten ou parten pas?*" ("So, Uncle, are we leaving or aren't we?") It's difficult to explain this Marseille humor that makes me laugh. First of all, there's that word *ounclé*, uncle, which is both condescending and slightly protective (like a young nephew to an uncle) and that casual way of considering the act of departure (very Marseille, hardly German, hardly soldier, not at all German soldier). It seemed like he was saying, "So, what's the decision?" Now what decision did that poor fellow have to make, buried under his luggage, his orders, and maybe even his doctrine. Hence, the laughter of the people on the train, and my own, slaves alike.

Sylvie: "I made five mistakes in my dictation." Since I give her some coins whenever she makes only one or two mistakes, I said, "So, no coins." "I know," she said. "And why five mistakes?" "There was a hard word." "What was it?" "*Intérieur*." (I'm very surprised.) "Yes," she said, "I put in an *h*," and she added, "I wanted to use two *l*'s." (I think that, in fact, seeing my surprise that she'd added an *h*, she was really saying, "Oh that's nothing, I almost put in two *l*'s," as if to say, "Imagine what could have happened!")

Charles: Slow, insensitive, narrow-minded, formerly an architect, he's forty years old, now my gardener, handyman. German, undoubtedly a Communist, at least a sympathizer. Gardener, but he cuts wood, goes to the farms for supplies, takes care of the rabbits and chickens. Pleasant enough tasks. Lives in the house, sleeps in the back of the library. Willing to help, loyal, good-natured, very devoted to me, to me and by extension to the whole house. I took him in stark naked, so to speak, dressed in rags. Now wears *new* clothes of mine recut to his size. Sleeps, slept with Mme. Ernst. Reads, takes notes, lives with us as an equal. Eats at my table, of course. And 600 francs a month, plus whatever he asks for anytime he asks for it.

A wasted day today. I read the detective novels that J. brought me at eleven o'clock. Decided to begin the text on Virgil tomorrow. The third act of *Voyage* seems short to me. The advantage of a quick resolution, but I must review the typed text as I correct it to make sure everything is clear enough. The possibility of fleshing out the scene with Donna Fulvia and the colonel, or finding a better exit for the colonel which, right now, is weak. That might come with writing the text on Virgil.

The legend. Radio National reported that Marcel Pagnol, sentenced in Aix at the film trial (that's true), paid me four million! (needless to say I wish it were true – the possibility then of donating the money to the town for a maternity ward at the hospital.) He didn't pay me anything and moreover, according to the figures of the experts, he owes me 1,500,000 francs, which he won't pay me. Dragging everything out as expected. As Marcel Pagnol must.

*November 9*

On this business of color, the best way to say it is that color must be made to play the same role (in film) that it plays in a painting. The painter hasn't put in the true color, or more accurately, he has *invented* (always the quarrel between true and false). What is annoying and *irritating* in color films is that the color is true. It must not be true. Just like Van Gogh paints the wheat field with a wide stroke of chrome yellow and doesn't care about capturing the glistening of the stalks other than through the white of the canvas (why? because in contemplating the actual wheat field his gaze was absorbed in the wonderful yellow of the ripe ears and the dazzling gray of the stalks seemed to him *white* in comparison.) Likewise, not to establish the truth, but the *sensual truth of relationships*. And for dramatic effect, maybe make the lips *green* and the eyes *red*. But that's another story.

Meyerowitz arrived late in the day. New troubles once again. Police, searches, fears, escapes, panic. What to do? Oh I was so, so thirsty, and what could I do but listen to endless moaning about the dangers he was in. Because I don't believe that there are new dangers. Nevertheless, for the ones that actually exist, I examine the issues seriously and try to find solutions. Seeing in all this the heroic side of salvation at any cost, I naturally propose heroic (and moreover, valuable) solutions to which M. raises amusing objections: Yes, but what about my piano? (a noble concern for work but a little bit Laurel and Hardy). I answer that there's some danger he'll have to give up on the piano. "But I don't think that's an immediate danger," he says. So I advise waiting. To which he replies, "Yes, but if they catch me tonight?" So now I don't know how to disentangle myself from all this. Is it serious? Unjustified panic? Collective fear? I don't know anymore. In the end I have to telephone B. to find out if M. could go to the A.'s at V. The comic side of each drama.

Mme. E's operation must be today.

And once more I didn't work today but read one of those infantile detective novels.

Reread the typed text of scene III of the third act Donna F. Julio. Satisfied enough with the tennis game. It returns us quite nicely to the first act. But I still think that the end of scene IV Donna F. Col. John is wrong. Fleshing it out a little and maybe (here must lie the secret) with another page or two – but very beautiful – in the last scene, and the third act would be perfect. Maybe that will come when I'm writing the text on Virgil. The distance, the shift to a different project, will cast fresh light on some inspiration, I think (I hope).

*November 10*

About half past noon sirens announced an alert. About one o'clock we could hear planes passing to the west. The alert ended at two. At three o'clock two German planes flew over us at very low altitude (50 or 60 meters). They came from the northeast and crossed in the direction of south-southwest. They didn't gain altitude as they approached the hills on the horizon and I kept them in sight as long as possible and I imagine that, if they followed the course of the Durance, they went around the rock of Saint-Eucher and are continuing their descent into the valley.

*November 11*

Last night another alert. The sirens went off at 2:30. I went to reassure my mother who was sleeping somewhere else and hadn't heard. What's more, what I took to be the beginning of the alert was the end. I hadn't heard the first warning (about one o'clock, I believe). This morning at nine o'clock, a great many planes passing over very high up.

The legend. This time it's *Le Petit Marseillais* reporting that I was paid four million! They seized the opportunity to draw a parallel with Verlaine who, they emphasized, died in poverty.

Began the text on Virgil. I'm rereading Stendhal's *Correspondance* from the beginning, when he was seventeen and was writing to his sister Pauline.

At 11:45 AM another alert. I was in town. Everyone ran. The police blew their whistles and made people go home, stopped cars, emptied cafés. I walked around trying to find Aline who should have been returning from school then. When I got to the Boulevard de la Plaine, it was already deserted and almost directly in front of the police station. I was not allowed to go on. Here I am and it's the finest weather in the world, bright and warm, full sun, calm, golden leaves, blue sky. No more noise, everyone lying low. Noon bells in a splendor of earthly Paradise.

The end of the alert sounded about three o'clock. At two, we could hear very far to the west the rumble of artillery fire or bombs. The train from Marseille that's supposed to arrive at 10 AM got in at 1 PM. The weather is fantastically beautiful.

Hung a Javanese cloth as a curtain in my south window because the morning sun is burning my paper and blinding me. Stained-glass window with a storm of flowers, leaves, purple and blue birds. I must go to the antique dealer and try to find a nice cloth to cover the west window on sunny afternoons when the same thing happens at the stroke of three.

Stendhal. *Correspondance*. Immediately surprised by the tone he uses to talk about his father to his sister Pauline. It's my papa, the papa. "Do you know if my papa had my books sent?" Nothing suggests the tone of Henry Brulard. The letter he writes from Goito near Mantova on February 24, 1801 (Letter 16 to his sister. The Divan, p. 41) is a marvel of romantic accuracy. Already present are almost all the minor characters and scenery of *La Chartreuse*. Lessons can be drawn here for appreciating his magnificent honesty. Here you can also see his brilliant interpretation. A minimum of lying, or more precisely the maximum, since it becomes unrecognizable in the reality he creates and nevertheless it operates on the senses like Van Gogh's big lie.


*November 12*


The alert sounded last night about ten o'clock, for the fourth time in twenty-four hours. Immediately we heard a great number of planes passing over so low that the windows shook. This morning the newspaper reported bombing in Modane and Annecy and one of the small villages in the Hautes-Alpes, La Fare-en-Champsaur. I wonder, why bomb Champsaur!? And it's not much easier to explain Annecy. In any case, the omens of birds seem to indicate troubled times for that region. On the whole, this is not so harmless. From now on, people are going to flee "for good" when the alert sounds. There are as many reasons to bomb Manosque as Annecy or La Fare. It's a question of luck or mood. We are in a sort of magic Froissart. The squadrons of planes don't seem to have any more military sense than the great armies of the Middle Ages. Once again the British are fighting in France, using the same methods as at the time of Bertrand de Guesclin. This was already apparent in Arabia in 1915 when Lawrence blew up the trains to Medina. That is, it's a kind of military sense but different from that of war schools, a different school of war in which everyone is considered hostile, in which the stronghold isn't distinguished from the remote farm. As this war grows old, nations rediscover their original natures. France today is just as spineless as during the Hundred Years' War. The English have reverted to the same period. The Italians have quite naturally rediscovered the Borgias and Orsinis. I have no basis for judging the Russians, but they can't be far from Tamerlane. The Germans are the mystery. They were nothing at that time. The Jews are precisely the Jews. The Jews of the Ghetto. You only have to look at their communities in Manosque or Forcalquier, clearly separate, voluntarily separate from the rest of the popu- lation. Republican achievements irremediably dead. Inevitable victor, as fleeting as that is: Communist ideas. Since the Middle Ages, in times like these, communities have formed. The ones to come will be more monstrous. The novelty is that they won't come from the peasants. On the contrary. Modern peasants, having become Koulaks almost everywhere, are a counterrevolutionary element against Communism. They are attached to property. But their natural egoism will no doubt keep them from joining forces. So who will form the opposition (I mean through violence and from the beginning)? Cowardly, small-minded bourgeoisie, caving in before being affected, immediately lying down, a bed for the whole Communist army to camp on from the outset. Trapped within their own egos, the peasants will hypocritically give in. But they will be an element in the struggle nevertheless because inwardly they will yield nothing of their ideas and positions based on property. They will only be able to fight, though, by dissolving away the Communist elements and over the long term. Communist violence will have no direct opponent. It is only over time, a generation, maybe even two or three (time for the Koulak spirit to be reborn in young peasants if it's destroyed in the old ones, and this rebirth happening spontaneously because it's natural), that French Communism, broken down from within by the natural chemistry of its peasantry, will once again become simple radical-socialist democracy. Nothing will come to nothing. The dead will be dead, a speck, that's all.

(This line of reasoning doesn't take into account America, where a radical-socialist structure might precipitate.)

More and more, I'm moved by the classics. I may come around to reading Corneille; that would be the last straw. In any case, very keen pleasure in reading La Bruyère and I'm beginning to understand Saint-Simon. A curious glance at the logic of Port-Royal. (My Javanese robe in my south window is a splendor this morning! Truly as beautiful as a beautiful stained-glass window.)

I went for a short walk this afternoon, and behind my house along the path that climbs the hill there was a woman spinning wool. She could have been Joan of Arc. She had made a distaff from an old umbrella handle. I stopped to talk to her, intrigued by the elegant gestures that effortlessly returned to her. She gave a little embarrassed laugh. She was making fun of herself, of our poverty, of so-called modern times, and her hands moved divinely.

Wonderful weather, hot, clear, but the wind is from the south and rain must be on the way. The Mont-d'Or olive orchards are like something out of Virgil.

The Church once wrote, speaking like a loving mother: "Everything for the people, but everything through the priests."

After the Church came the Monarchy: "Everything for the people, but everything through the Prince."

The doctrinarians: "Everything for the people, but everything through the bourgeoisie."

The Jacobins did not change the principle by changing the formula: "Everything for the people, but everything through the State."

It is always the same governmentalism, the same Communism."

Proudhon (*Souvenirs d'un révolutionnaire*)

Clemenceau to Lloyd George:
"The day after the armistice I find you the enemy of France."
"Well, isn't that our politics as usual!"

(*Grandeurs et misères d'une victoire*)

Nothing is noble but pacifism. And you better believe, M. Montherlant, that it requires the nerves of a toreador and the strength of an athlete. And much more courage than war. I made war in 1914 well enough. *I haven't been able to make peace in 1939.*

Albert arrived. He's the boyfriend of Marguerite, the maid who preceded Barbara. One morning my mother-in-law heard noise in Marguerite's room. My wife went up and found Albert hidden in the space between the bed and the wall. He was spending nights there. They were fired. Albert has always liked me. He's from Thionville. He talks as if his tongue isn't completely detached from his palate. He's handsome in the way of young film stars. He's had much success with women. He tells me his troubles. He thinks that Marguerite cheated on him with an Italian soldier – I wouldn't wish on anyone what happened to me, he says darkly. Of course I agree with him, but what can you do. He told me that he was shaking, that he lost his head, and then he beat her, and then he sat up with her all night. It seems she was spitting blood. Marguerite cried and told him that she was going to die, that she had only six months, and that he must let her do what she wanted if he loved her. He asks me for advice and I give it. He took Marguerite to Marseille to the doctor's. There's nothing wrong with her. But he also tells me that M., out of jealousy, beat a girl that he had looked at, and then she fainted in his arms. Impossible to render the tone of these confidences, mixed with declarations of love that he offers me, or the declarations of love that Marguerite makes through him. Finally I tell him to come back sometime if he needs to get things off his chest, and he gives me a bag of tobacco as a parting gift and leaves.

*November 13*

*Stendhal.* I was belaboring the point. I didn't need to find all the terms of endearment he uses for his father in the letters to Pauline. He writes to him on March 3, 1803 (Letter 36, *Divan*, vol. I, p. 109) and you couldn't ask for more humility, love, submission, or tenderness. So much so that it's clear: this is hypocrisy. Impossible to love someone with whom one uses this tone of complete inferiority. Especially when the writer is ambitious, and even though he has just written to Pauline that among the men of genius in Grenoble their father ranks first. It's obvious what he really thinks of him. What he will say in H.B.

I wrote so hurriedly last evening about Albert's confidences that what I wrote about Marguerite may seem ambiguous. Albert, who considers me his friend, said this in an awkward and exaggerated way (what I jokingly called his declarations of love); and it's exactly the same with regard to what I call Marguerite's declarations of love. She was just surprised that I showed her kindness and understanding, accustomed as she was to everyone's harsh treatment of her. So A. told me awkwardly that she remembers me with warm feelings. That's all there is to it. I have no interest in women. Especially not her. For me it's just as though she didn't exist. Except to give her a hundred francs when she went to Marseille to see a doctor. And with me she was always very respectful and slightly dumbstruck. Yes, it's true, women (in plural) really don't interest me. It would surprise me if there wasn't some legend about this.

Alain Cuny, in Paris one day, said something to me about it – at the corner of Rue Bonaparte, along the Seine. The truth is very different. Yes, I'm sensual, very much so, but pathologically faithful. I become attached and never again detach myself. Infidelity is physically impossible for me, while I might be enormously physical straightaway with whatever I love. Romanticism. The need for feeling. And then delights. The rest, no. I really do prefer a pipe and solitude.

The mistral again. Not very cold, as when it begins and will last for several days. Skies heavy with the green marshes of the southern gulfs. Despite the wind, clouds motionless, so very high up. Over Marseille, in that direction, brilliant cumulus against a background of murky gray sky.

Office peaceful, cozy, warm; magnificent morning light through the Javanese stained-glass.

At noon, bucolic lunch, the two farmers from Margotte and Criquet were there, having come with fresh supplies. There's always some disappointment. The distillation of the marc at Margotte that should have provided forty liters of brandy only produced twenty-four. At Criquet where it should have produced another twenty (the same weight), it provided eighteen. Large Mme. Bonnefoy sat next to little Salomé and they both ate our lentils. I had equipped them each with a little horse and carriage with rubber tires to come to Manosque. Regarding horses, Salomé has taken it upon himself to sell the Criquet horse, which is sick. But at first it was to be about 80,000, now Salomé hopes to get 60,000, but he claims he has a buyer offering 30,000. All this small talk is not insignificant. Nothing a farmer says is random. Well, in any case, Salomé, who was shoeless, shirtless, and penniless two years ago and to whom I gave a 400,000 franc advance (without requiring anything in exchange) (current rate, but real outlay 150,000) has a bank account now, and Mme. Bonnefoy has the air of a lady. So much the better. And they both bring me fresh supplies on the dot.

The lawyer paid me 3,500 francs. The balance from the sale of Uncle's printing press, which my father and mother spent all their savings to buy in 1909 – 4,000 francs I believe, and they went into debt for 7 or 8,000 I think. I remember that as soon as we sat down to eat, all anyone talked about were the machines, the paper cutter, etc., and whenever my father and mother could talk without Uncle hearing, there were tears and wailing on my mother's side – especially as the end of the month approached when payments came due – I still remember Gonelle's features and name. And on my father's side, a kind of resigned sadness. Because Uncle continued to get drunk regularly and the beautiful work he did at first deteriorated. Finally, seven or eight years ago, I forced Uncle to sell. He was no longer working – he never worked – and he was still getting drunk. It was Rico who bought it, 20,000 francs, I think (which would have come in handy back then), paying 10,000 down, with the other 10,000 to be paid in installments handled by the lawyer. These 3,500 francs are the last of those installments. I gave the money to my mother. Not that she needs anything of course, but I know that it makes her happy and it makes sense that this money is returned to her. She had enough worries when she was up to her neck in debt, with her ironing as her only means of income and her old shoemaker husband upstairs in his lonely workshop.

At three o'clock, Maman comes up to my office. I hear her feeling her way through Barbara's room, then her blind steps, and she knocks. She's brought her small purse. I tell her to sit down and catch her breath. Then her funds must be organized. She has me count and stack the thousand-franc notes (she already had three from her old-age pension). Since she's blind, I have her touch the bills and I tell her that one of the recently issued bills is smaller than the others. She counts; there are now five thousand-franc notes. The 500-franc notes are in another pocket. There are four of them. Five, because I discover another one hidden in separate pocket of her wallet. She's reassured, she thought she'd lost it. That makes 7,500 francs total. "If you didn't have to pay inheritance tax," she says, "I'd invest them!" She's happy, she laughs, she's in good spirits. This is all perfectly useless. She wraps her wallet in a handkerchief. She tucks it into her purse. She puts the purse strap over her arm and I walk her down to the first floor. She says to me, "switch off the lights, I'm going to go through Mémé's room." I go back to my office.


*November 14*

I'm trying hard to record as precisely as possible the most or-dinary everyday events. My taste for invention can lead to an obscure lyricism. I need somewhere private, not meant to be published, where I can practice scales, exercise my fingers on tougher disciplines. I must try to express these small everyday events quickly and in the most accurate way possible. Stick close to and describe what happens; the most commonplace, invent nothing. Acquire that style, if possible. It'll at least allow me to feel my way maybe for two or three years. But I enjoy this effort, so if, by the end of that time, I've only acquired mastery over myself (if invention no longer masters me, which is always the case now), it will have been worth it. After nearly twenty years of work, I've still not managed to write a true book. I haven't worked hard enough. These calisthenics may build my muscles. To date, everything I've done lacks depths. I will only be able to lie well (truly invent) when I learn to be very true. Submit to the object. Find the style. An analytical art.

*Stendhal.* He detests Mounier. He writes him very long letters, obsequious in their fawning and pretending to be direct. Mostly he writes about his feminine conquests, which he invents or exaggerates or turns to his advantage. He depicts himself as a rogue, disenchanted conqueror, a Don Juan. Harassed by women. In fact, he isn't writing to Mounier, he couldn't care less about Mounier. He's writing so that Mounier will show these letters to his sister Valentine with whom he's in love. And Mounier will never do that. The rogue out-rogued.

Barometer very low this evening. No wind. Heavy black clouds rising from the south and west. Already all I can see of the sky is murky and formless. A coating of mud. The signs of a storm, of rough weather, any violent shift, give me great physical pleasure. And when it breaks, my only fear is seeing it end. Evening blue almost black, a lid. The chestnut leaves trembling, the branches still. The arrival of these great things that have nothing to do with men. Escape from the petty.

*November 15*

What is the meaning of André Gide's silence? He was in Tunis when the English took it. Since then, not a word. There's the radio. There are friends who speak up for you. There are those who proudly declare their allegiance. He was already partisan, which could prevent him from taking sides again. Why he doesn't speak up himself can be explained to some degree: he's too honest to want to play spokesman in an armed conflict. But if he's in English territory, he must have relations with the authorities. And if they are friendly relations, it's surprising that the authorities haven't used Gide's name to their advantage for propaganda purposes. It would be significant if Radio Algiers reported that M. Gide was siding with the English. They used the name of Max-Pol Fouchet and the Fontaine staff. Nevertheless, nothing. Dead silence. Could it be the Russians?

Despite my barometer, a very fine cold sun this morning.
But once again this afternoon, overcast.

We can't give France a finer gift than to destroy its great cities with the bomb. Imagine the flood of ready cash pouring in from all sides of the globe for reconstruction. It would be the time of plenty and easy money. We are establishing a low pressure system here that will make us the center of a money cyclone after the war.

And just wait for all our industries that converted their factories for the war to *write off* their expenditures for machinery.

Satisfied with the beginning what I'm writing on Virgil. I'm getting there in a roundabout way. I want to be interesting. I'm incapable of saying anything new about Virgil or anything scholarly, and I don't know Latin. At the beginning of these poetic pages, simply to do my poetic work. The sentence has *number* (what I've been seeking for a long time – succeeded in *Pour saluer Melville*) and I'm sure that up to this point (four pages written) it reads not only interestingly but makes the reader eager for what comes next. But it's still the art of summary. Up to this point.

*November 16*

Everything's going smoothly with *Virgile*. I'm enjoying it. I think I'm going to call it "Jardins d'Armide." Make it – if possible – a kind of poetics. Above all, I would like it to be read and appreciated as an adventure story. The best part is that, for the moment, I'm enjoying writing the story as if I were telling it to myself.

At noon an alert, thirty minutes later, all over. Nothing, as usual.

Kerolyr, who got a ride with the Forcalquier Roads and Bridges engineer, came to see me this morning. It's been three years since I've seen him. He's still making photographs of space in his observatory up there, but, he says, the more beautiful they are, the more of a pain in the neck. If he had had help, he could have been the one to do the photographic index of the Herschel nebulae. A month ago I received a letter from him with a 500 franc note. What is this 500 franc note, I wrote back. He told me that I had lent it to his daughter, and today he came to see if I could lend it back to him again, which I did. Took advantage of the opportunity to mention Meyerowitz to the engineer, who will mention him to the sub-prefect. I spoke in glowing terms, as they could play beautiful music together. If M. is patient and takes my advice, I can arrange a very peaceful and safe situation for him in Forcalquier; he'll risk nothing whatsoever. Hardly had I finished writing this when the bell rings and it's Meyerowitz. He's found lodgings in Saint-Maime. He tells me that Kerolyr is "comestible" but that X is a "parody of Joan of Arc," and that she's "anti-erectable." I tell him that between Kerolyr, the engineer, and the sub-prefect, he's already safe enough in Forcalquier and even in Saint-Maime. But on a new front, M. has already seen the Saint-Maime priest. Played his organ, charmed and disgusted the postman, and moved into the lodgings near the grade crossing. Everything has to be redone. Also, M. met Auréas's daughter and has managed to get himself invited to Aubenas. Mme. B. has sent him the key to her house in Vachères. I wonder what the hell I'm doing mixed up in this business!

*November 17*

Sylvie is studying history. Her mother has her recite her lesson. What is a border? Sylvie: It's a line where there's an enemy on either side.

*November 18*

Snow this morning on all the hills. Manosque has become black with smoke as during my childhood. It hangs heavily. Delightful rain. Dark nests of snow squalls lie to the south near Marseille. Snow here always comes from the south. Snow from Corsica. It might even be called Italian snow. Beautiful winter. Magnificent winter. This delightful annoyance.

Calm here. Yesterday Michel came for his weekly chat. He came from Aix where he'd gone to deliver Chulan's horse. A racehorse belonging to Saint-Cyr that had to be turned over to the draft board. M. rode the horse to Aix. A story from "Merovingian times." Going up to Venelles, he said, he dismounted to eat. He gave the horse free rein and it grazed beside him. But the roads where the tar wasn't completely worn away were slippery for horseshoes and he yearned for a dirt road the whole journey, a simple dirt road. Now that would have been an improvement, because it would have let him trot and he could have stopped worrying about his horse falling if he let up on the reins.

In one village in the Hautes-Alpes, the farmers who relied on horses to work the fields simply plowed up all the roads that ran through their area. They didn't want to risk broken knees.

Real life rests a hand gently on my arm, like Socrates's daemon.

There are two or three very good pages to be written right between John's lines and Donna Fulvia's lines at the end of the third act, and then *Voyage* will be perfect.

Three vivid, romantic, Stendhalian pages on the real risks that Julio *runs* and that consequently D.F. *is going to run, the transport of love.* Then it will be done.

I spoke too soon about the calm. Telephone call at noon. It's

Meyerowitz! There's a plot afoot at the boarding house! A gendarme accused him of wild partying, told him he better get to work as a farmhand, and took his papers. He's in a panic. Once again, all is lost. The gendarme was rough. And then, he (Meyerwitz) says, "Have you seen Mme. Régnier about the piano, have you worked on *Bout de la route* (which he wants to make into an opera) for me?" I reassured him. I'm gnashing my teeth a little.

In the afternoon I heard Élise below raising her voice as when there's an argument. I went down a bit later and asked what was going on. It seems that Charles didn't want to go get the coal. (We missed our turn for 400 kilograms.) Élise gets upset easily with the help and can't make anyone listen to her without shouting. But it's true, Charles has been acting strangely for some time. What's up with him? He's part of the family. He even gets the same dessert as the children. He works about three hours a day and what is that work? Going for milk and the paper, splitting a little wood, when it's nice out going to the farms by bicycle from time to time for supplies. I would easily and happily do all his tasks myself. So what's up?

I went to the funeral of my cousin Odette's brother-in-law. A farmer's funeral. Quite noble, handled like the business of peasants. When I got back I found a summons from Liotard, the examining judge, for Thursday, November 25 in Digne at two o'clock "as witness in the matter about which he will be given knowledge." Haven't the least idea what this is about. But this coming Thursday worries me especially.

To get my revenge, I'm ordering a few beautiful books that I've wanted, *Apocalypse de saint Sever*, by Ariosto, illustrated by Doré, the Bible also illustrated by Doré, and then a standard edition of Maurice Scève from Garnier. I already have an Ariosto from 1603 and one from 1586, both illustrated with woodcuts and a little Ariosto in ten volumes, text and translation on facing pages, that I'm using to learn Italian. I also have a beautiful Dante from 1564 (the 43rd edition) with commentaries by Landino and Sansovino that I'm planning to read to learn Italian. And all worries become secondary.

*November 19*

American progress and comforts. Imitation snow sprayed in the streets by municipal vehicles, the nights of Christmas too mild, "Happy Christmas!" nevertheless. Who would accuse us of forgetting traditions? Sharp reaction against the dumbstruck, admiring expectations of the majority. You don't like them? Yes, of course I do, and that's why I don't make the mistake of telling them a few plain truths.

Wonderful dark weather. North wind, cold, rain. Today, truly, weather for a bed warmer. Last evening I was reading an old issue of the *Revue de Paris*, pages from the journal of Julien Green. At first Gide says to him, "You'll have to choose a side, Communist or Fascist." And shortly after that Gide says to him, "You do well in not choosing between Communists and Fascists especially since it's the same thing. You're apolitical, stay there." In between, the trip to the U.S.S.R. It's impossible for me to stop thinking about Gide being in English territory and keeping quiet and especially that others are keeping quiet for him. Strange conclusions to be drawn from that.

Is Meyerowitz going to muck up my peace today? Seven o'clock in the evening. The bell rings. Meyerowitz of course. He doesn't dare come up. He has a short letter delivered to me that says, "Between train and bus. I almost don't dare face you. If you aren't anti-Jewish, I'll be the one to make you so. Even if I transformed myself into Saint Cécile, even then, I could never make up for all the damned trouble that my iniquitous being causes you. I am ashamed! May I sit down with you for a minute? Your ignoble M." I say, "Have him come up." I learn that the boarding house plot is limited to the complaints of women with sons doing compulsory work for the S.T.O., and who were scandalized seeing M. walking about impervious. He hasn't been "retiring as a violet." Does that come as any surprise? Through Ch. and the Marseille prefecture, I'm devising a way to have the ears boxed of the Forcalquier warrant officer. But above all, M. must be discreet, I tell him again, discreet, and he must walk on tiptoe, there are sick people in the house, damn it! Revenge. As he's leaving, I ask, "what will your fiancée do in Saint-Maime for Christmas?" "There are two hotels," he says. "Yes, but she's going to get bored." It comes out so naturally that he explodes, "With me!?" That's all. "That's diabolical," he says. Basically, he's not a bad fellow.

*November 20*

*Realism*. André Antoine is wrong and that must be said if we want to find the elements for a renaissance poetics: it's performing before the audience that's true. Wholly facing the audience. Never turning your back to them, never performing from behind, that is *the truth*. As for the real, as for realism, if we want go the whole way with it, it must be in *the space*, and not *the plane*. Then, yes, that's real. As for the rest, it simply makes for voyeurism, looking through a keyhole, indiscretion. Don't bother, indiscretion is already part of the artwork. Modern art murdered by Antoine's so-called discovery. Parisian invention. As for true reality, there's nothing more unreal. Thérive and the populists real? No. Dabit real? No. Petty. The real is not petty. Nobody can make me believe (it's physically impossible) that there isn't a milligram of gold sludge in a worker at Renault or in the Soviet's Poutekoff iron and steel factories. And a milligram, even a hundredth of a milligram, even a trace, and their whole theory of realism shatters into a tale from *A Thousand and One Nights*. Reality imitates life? What life? At the root of this error, ignorance of true human nature. What arrogance they must have to decide that life is this pettiness. False scholars, but followed as such. Clearly this is easier to understand than true knowledge. Parisian prophets, another great subject for a good laugh.

*November 21*

One can't say Germany or Russia anymore. It doesn't mean anything. You have to say National Socialism or Communism. For England and America, it's Democracy. But France still doesn't have a proper name on the political map of this war. How lovely if it had a proper name (in literal sense of the word proper). Just now I said National Socialism and not Fascism. *Fascio* is Italian and there has never been an Italy, a political Italy (on the international level), that's a mirage (a fraud).

*Sunday.* I'd like to be in Delphi, boarding with a family in some small Greek village. The sacred olive trees caressing my gray hair and reading Aeschylus's *Prometheus* today in the great empty theatre set into the hill like an ammonite. That's out of the question: I go to the movies: Raimu, *Monsieur La Souris*. I come home. I enjoyed it.

Rarely do I give what I promised. Often I give less or nothing, but even more often, much more often, "too much." So much so that what I give no longer bears any relationship to what was asked of me and what I promised; and thus, what I give doesn't count, and I still *owe* what I promised. In either case, it's terribly awkward and more in the second case than the first. *All* my enemies are the result of this. All my friends, even my most dear (and only) friends have gone and left me because of this. But one. I must acknowledge him, Auguste Michel. His gratitude has never wavered and he has never tired of it. Steadfast loyalty, and I say to all of you, Lucien Jacques, you as well, that Michel has known me since kindergarten and it's certainly not through knowledge that one tires of me but through pride.

General rule by which I could be judged: I never make *a profit* from what I've promised (even when I give less, or nothing).

*November 23*

The examining judge in Digne is taking his time. After summoning me to Digne on Thursday the 25th – it's a long trip and disrupts my plans – he sent word today that instead of the 25th he want me on Monday the 29th. I rescheduled my engagements for exactly that date. I responded immediately by telegram and by letter, sharply and firmly. I will not go to Digne on Monday.


*November 24*

A visit from the Forcalquier sub-prefect last evening. He's a poet. He won the Guillaume-Apollinaire award. Speaking of things in general, he told me that the police are afraid. Thus, impunity for all acts of terrorism, no matter what they are. But, in my opinion, that means everyone is free to murder and plunder. Not just the Communists, but also the enemies of the Communists, and even just plain crooks. That's when the idea of revolution will lose its virginity. A few big *gratuitous* murders, followed by *very conspicuous* thefts with as many horrifying details as possible, rapes, hangings of small children, crude and sadistic cruelties, with *Communism* carefully written all over them, and there you have it, the idea defiled. It's a wonder that the Communists aren't suspicious. Because the police could easily pull this off. Or a kind of Ku Klux Klan, vigilantes assembled by a handful of the firmly resolved (and these could be sons, brothers, of the murdered). It would only take ten or twelve of them, strong, brave, armed, masked, quick, to attack a small town some evening where there have been murders attempted by Communists. They could massacre with impunity one or two Communist families well-known there, hang them from trees along the boulevard, and vanish, quick, masked, mysterious. The Avengers! A huge sensation no doubt. Especially if they were cunning enough to give their attack a romantic edge, the mark of Zorro. Very dangerous, because one initial success would be enough to make huge numbers, in every country, district, town, and village, want to play, begin to play, Zorro.

The works of mine that Grasset argued against publishing in 1929 and the following years are now the ones saving Grasset Editions through their reissues and sales.

Gray weather, snow and cold. I can't stop thinking about Lucien Jacques. What stupidity, because if it's not stupid, it's tragic. He must have drawn the wrong conclusions from me not wanting to go with him to Besson's or Martin's during his business with the

Contadour. But if I didn't go with him, it was for other, purely personal, reasons, and to stay out of his way, because his complaints, in my presence, could have been taken on a whole other level.

*November 25*

Maman came into my office to have me cut her fingernails on her right hand. She sits down to rest in front of my fire, valiantly calming her asthma. Her breathing is so labored that I take big breaths myself as if the air I so easily inhale could aerate her. Then I cut her nails. She lets out the usual little cries when I cut the corners. Her nails are brittle as stone. Then she does the nails on her left hand by herself. But she asks me, "Are these alright? – No, they aren't cut very well, wait, I'm going have you fix them. – I used to be able to cut them very well, but now I can't anymore." Then, while I cut them, she makes little girlish sounds, laughing. "Here, now file my nails," and she gives me small butterfly tweezers on which there's a kind of file. And she goes on forever gently filing her nails, dozing before my fire.

Of course Meyerowitz came by last evening with a terrible torrent of new catastrophes. Gestapo. Mme. Schweim is a spy. Two giants with machine guns arrested M. Folk and his son, who deserved it, he adds. I take all this seriously and advise him to take refuge in Aubenas and then go stay at the B.'s house in Vachères since they've given him their key. But immediately there's the question of whether a piano can be delivered to Aubenas, and then, what will he do in Vachères. "I'll go crazy," he says. So I ask him if it's really a question of life and death as he claims. "Oh, yes!" he says. So, in my opinion, now's not the time to worry about a piano. Louis Maurel is staying with us right now, having returned sick after being held in Koenigsberg. I have to ask them both into my office at once, since it's the only heated room in the house (except the kitchen).

Terrible wind. Under the sun, the cloudless sky is black as ink.

The examining judge in Digne had an officer deliver a polite letter in which he invites me to set the date for the hearing myself.

Louis Maurel told me that when he arrived in East Prussia, they had summoned the farmers in the area to come select prisoners, as slaves were selected in Cervantes's time or, more recently, in America before the Civil War. The farmers sized them up, feeling their arms and legs, *looking at their teeth*. A horrible ceremony. Hard to pardon. Absolutely unpardonable. Despite the fact that, later, German soldiers coming from other areas in preparation for the attack on Russia behaved humanely toward them, especially at Christmas. Impossible to accept the slave market. Maurel tells me about the feudalism of the Prussian country squires and the vast snow-covered plains surrounded by a black crown of distant fir forests where he went by sleigh to cut wood. No matter what happens, those slave markets must not be forgotten.

Charles is nervous today; according to a note that appeared in the newspaper, the German authorities consider him a deserter. I reassured him.

*November 28*

The trouble with Charles started suddenly yesterday morning. Impossible to talk about it yet, whatever comes of this business. It meant that I had to ask Salomé for a small favor. It didn't require much bravery. This morning Salomé arrived with the weekly supplies and you could see right away that he was doing it grudgingly. Did I hesitate to take on even greater risks than his when it was a matter of rescuing Francis? He talks about that business like an idiot. But that wouldn't matter at all if I hadn't noticed the truth about the business with Ch. Which let me see clearly the truth about Salomé. I wrote what appears above before sitting down to lunch with Salomé, where I vowed to give him a piece of my mind. It was Élise who came to tell me that he was refusing to help Ch. So I saw Salomé at lunch and I didn't mention the matter throughout the meal. I reminded him incidentally and tangentially of all the favors I'd recently done for him. Then after lunch I shook his hand and said I was going to work. He followed me into the hall and told me that, regarding the business with Ch., he would do what I'd asked him – let me repeat, I asked him only to play a passive role. When I reminded him of this, he said, "Every time I ask you for this sort of favor (I'm really good about it, this is the first time I've asked! And probably the last!), there's no risk in it for you. And moreover, every time, you lay all the blame on me." As soon as this business is a little less fresh, I'll use it for practicing those scales that are teaching me to stick as close as possible to the truth. An excellent exercise, it's all here: the stark drama, the egoism of these extraordinary times we're living in.

Meyerowitz telephoned at noon. Of course he's at Vachères and complaining: it's sad, it's lonely, he's never been so unhappy, I need to call B., they haven't made arrangements for the key. He's annoyed, no one wants to make his meals (that's more serious). He has never been in such a sad situation. But in passing he tells me that the sub-prefect has been extraordinarily kind to him on my recommendation.

One.

Two. Mme. Ernst, released from the hospital after her successful operation (which cost me 7,000 francs) comes to tell me that she has no more money. Neither do I. I'm waiting. Maybe I'm about to receive some.

Three. R., whose wife has been ill for years (some kind of stomach pains, kidneys, those mysterious women's complaints, I believe), comes to ask me to telephone Dr. Aviérinos in Marseille so that he can make an appointment to have his wife examined on Tuesday. Once again, no money. On my recommendation, Aviérinos will examine her free of charge. But there's still the taxi to Marseille. And the hospital, if necessary.

Four. L.D. and family don't seem to have more than 250 francs. Once again, they need money.

All at the same time, and I really don't have any. At five o'clock, another call from Meyerowitz, anxious, panic-stricken, lost, he received a telegram from the B.'s, he has the key, he's going to the A.'s house, they'll give him room and board. He's upset. But this is the hour when I must bring the rabbits in and while he's on the phone it's getting dark, and I tell him to hurry up. He tells me he doesn't like that. I go fetch the rabbits. The grass that Barbara brought is wet. I go to pick a few cabbage leaves and for each cage I add some thyme and a handful of barley. At first I see only two hens, but the third is hidden in the egg trough. I return out of remorse and give extra rations to the mother rabbits with babies bunnies. They are calm around me and sniff my hands. They are very hungry. Since Ch. left, I'm in charge of gathering grass for them, cutting wood in the morning, and looking after the farmyard. Not a minute to work today.

Henry is sick. Élise just came from his house. He had telephoned. It seems he has a horrible boil on his little toe. His leg is swollen up to the knee, and black. The doctor advised squeezing the boil to drain the puss. Henry's wife doesn't dare. I'll go tomorrow morning. Very afraid that this could be bad for him, at his age and with serious diabetes. Henry is Jourdan of *Colline* and Janet of *Colline* was his father-in-law, Jean Pic, known as Janet. It was witnessing the long agony of Janet's alcoholism that gave me the idea for writing *Colline*. I listened patiently to Janet's ramblings. I kept him company, he used to say. It was in the early days of my marriage. Henry has known Élise since her birth and used to bounce her on his knee. Élise just told him that he was expected here for Christmas, that there might be a turkey. He told her, "I'll make crutches and be there."

Last night I dreamed about Lucien Jacques. How stupid! Me, too!

*November 29*

Anatole France's revival awaits the end of the war. Although it may apparently tend toward revolutionary extremes, that period will be radical socialist at its core. Radical-socialism is the purest expression of all that revolutions become. The tadpole loses its tail, the Jacobin loses his guillotine, it's the law of evolution, and thus we have radical socialism. Russia is radical socialist at present; only the eastern part.

Meyerowitz telephones at ten. Everything's going very well, it seems.

Charles's tasks are gradually becoming part of my own work. Gave the rabbits their food and lovely grass. They are friendly and delightful. I already know their habits, cage by cage. The hens are a bit more difficult. After that, I split the wood for the day and eventually came up here where my beautiful Javanese stained glass produces a delicate amber light and immediately I have clarity for work. Last evening, after all the problems, I was able to clear one long hour of calm (understood in flashes the calm of Mipam at the Ngarong monastery). I had arranged the *Apocalypse de saint Sever* under my lamp; an immense calm issued from the large folio format. The massiveness plays a very important role. With each turn of the enormous pages, the eye receives the impression of a giant portion of food being offered to it. Even without reading. If, in addition, there is Froissart or Ariosto or the wonderful images of the Apocalypse, then gradually the cloister burrows into itself like a conch, surrounded by its galleries, forests, precipices, and mountains.

*November 30*

This evening, a desperate call from Meyerowitz. He went to Forcalquier. According to what I could understand of what he told me in veiled terms, he's especially high on the wanted list. He's even afraid that he will be picked up at Vachères. The Auréases don't seem to have greeted him with tears of joy, and I understand that. But now all I can do is give him advice, and what should I tell him? Stay at V. and go into hiding if necessary? That's what a man would do.

Once again, major money worries that keep me awake at night. My taxes are coming due. I'm going to find myself stripped bare facing a payment of 80,000 francs to the tax department. On the other hand, the business with Ch. is sorted out, for the time being.

*December 1*

"…joyfully fleeing a vile country." (Baudelaire)

I'm reading an excerpt from *Scènes de la vie future* in an old *Revue de Paris*. Could it be that Duhamel is a great man?

Last evening, four phone calls, one after another, from Meyerowitz. I don't know. He must already stand out like a green monkey at Vachères. Finally he announced that he was coming to see me this morning. But he wanted to come as early as possible. "But what time?" "Seven." "That's when I split wood and afterwards I feed the rabbits." "I'll wait for you in the library." "Yes, but it'll take me two hours." "It'll take you two hours to do that?" "Yes, because I enjoy it." "Giono! Could you try not to enjoy it tomorrow morning?!" (Is this the tone of a desperate man? Is there the least sincerity in it? Does it ring true and clear? No.) I answer, "I forgot to tell you that I use the bathroom during those two hours as well." "Okay, " he says, "then I'll come at ten o'clock, that'll be fine."

Meyerowitz arrives, touches my cheek lightly with his finger to see if I've shaved, he tells me a long story about sleeping standing up, pushed around by two giant, crude and vindictive soldiers, he asks me for money, he asks me for fats, he asks me what on earth he's supposed to do at Vachères, and where will he go if they track him down at Vachères, and what he's supposed to do without a piano, he asks me for a letter of reference for M. de Lombardon, he asks to borrow my favorite books (which I flatly refuse him). I get a phone call. I leave him alone for a moment. When I come back, he's kneeling in front of the bookcase where I keep all the books I love and he's pawing through them and he says, "Can I take this one?" I tell him no. The phone again, again I come back, he's rummaging through them. Nothing to be done this time, he leaves with *La Passion du Palatinus*.

*December 2*

Ch. returned last evening. The danger is not yet passed and threatens him at every turn. An inspector from the Les Mées camp came to warn me that M. is also facing real dangers.

*December 3*

Bombing in Toulon, 600 dead, and yesterday, bombing in Marseille, 50 dead. A young boy, eleven years old, arrived here from Toulon. He doesn't speak anymore. He trembles. He's lost the use of all his senses and is left with only the sense of fear. M. Y. came to ask us for Mémé's rooms for his daughter and his wife. Apart from this instinct for self-preservation, M. Y. has little more reason than a drum, he rumbles when he's beaten and you can make him rumble as you like. He rumbles the call to arms just as well as the retreat, and you can even get funny farting noises out of him.

There's a film to be made out of the story of Jeanne de Buis who appears in chiaroscuro in the *Virgile* that I'm writing. Very easy to do. In color (the slaughterhouse) but I see it all entirely as night. Nocturnal film. The importance of nocturnes in what I'm writing. It could be beautiful, the color of night.

Meyerowitz telephones. He asks me if I have a car to take him to Marseille. I tell him that when I go there I take the train (I've never owned a car), then, in a soft voice, "Couldn't you ask a friend for me?" That, in my opinion, is very beautiful. Biblical! M. adds, "Have you gotten the money?" (but I seem to be inventing a character).

*December 4*

Yesterday evening, Albert came back to talk to me about his love, his jealousy, and to ask my advice. This fellow seems decent and honest, completely without guile. He's strong, and has the goodness and faithfulness of the strong. He detests lies. He's sincerely distressed when I show him that despite everything, he's obliged to lie at least twenty times a day. He brings me a bit of fluid for my lighter and some stones and he tells me that I have another present coming. He keeps me in suspense respectfully but as if with a child, because apparently this is the anniversary of the day when he first came to see me. And he gives a bag of tobacco.

Telegram: Audré Maurin, Élise's first cousin, who has been in a concentration camp for three years for being a Communist, has just been released and put under house arrest in Manosque. No doubt at his request because we've been helping him throughout with money and packages. He must believe that this is the Klondike. He'll arrive Tuesday, three days from now.

I read in Froissart that the king of England presented the king of Cyprus with a ship that was docked at Sandwich, called *The Catherine*. That ship cost 12,000 francs. What could 12,000 francs buy you now: an overcoat on the black market or maybe even a ham!

*December 4*

Went out this evening to go to the post office. Coming back, it was raining, and I ran into Durieux who was leaving the mine. He stopped and asked me if I would be home tomorrow. "Yes." "Then I'll send René over (that's his youngest son), he still has some books for you to sign (he came over just two weeks ago to have me sign four books). We would like to have all of them," Durieux says, "My wife says that we must have them all. They still cost 300 francs." I tell him, "I promised René that I'd give him one for Christmas." "Ah!" says Durieux, "It's *Le Poids du ciel* that I want, and *Moby Dick*. I want them all. I just read *Précisions*. I've read it three times." "Send René tomorrow morning." "Thank you."

Nothing touches me more deeply. This is an honest-to-goodness miner. His oldest son went as far as the baccalauréat. René is a beautiful child, solid and serious, with the eyes of a doe and the mouth of a girl. Durieux is *from up north*, near Lille. Has been in Manosque for over twenty years. I come home feeling encouraged and responsible for doing what I do well.

*December 6*

Last night an alert at about eleven o'clock. Four or five break-ins in just a few days here. Potatoes, perfume, and money were stolen from the houses. In Laragne, two masked men armed with machine guns robbed the tax collector at four o'clock in the afternoon. In Banon, four masked men held up the Apt-Banon bus and stole tobacco. At the same time, other masked men in Banon hijacked a tank truck carrying 1,000 liters of gasoline. The Wild West. Farms are being set on fire. Gradually, gangs like Cartouche's are going to form that will abandon patriotism for profit, pure and simple. I've cleaned and loaded the small revolver. It can't do much harm, but there it is. I'm going to ask Gaston for a larger caliber. In any case, simply with regard to drama, it's all good material for *Les Grands chemins*. The cloak-and-dagger novel of modern times. If I could only be Ponson de Terrail! Well, I'm going to try my best.

Yesterday read quickly (that's the only way to read it) a volume from *Hommes de bonne volonté* by Jules Romains. *Vorge contre Quinette*. We sense there the fifty-year-old man, sexually exhausted and drooling impotently over his young secretary. Long-winded, petit-bourgeois, minor eroticism. I prefer the genuine eroticism of Malraux. He has balls. An annoying book, badly written, badly constructed if at all, meaningless. Sentences like this one: "Above *reigned* a corridor...." (A corridor that reigns!) Jules Romains must have read somewhere that Balzac wrote badly and he believed it. Also at the very beginning of the volume (second sentence) there's this incredibly affected sentence that says the opposite of what it ought to say ("it was not without having to overcome some repugnance that he decided to purchase that smock the other day"). College student coolness. Skilled juggler who hides his blunders with cleverness. Total lack of simplicity, sincerity, truth. Oh yes, he ought to have taken lessons from Ponson de Terrail.

Ch. must leave for longer this time. The thing that seemed settled remains a danger. No more news from Meyerowitz. Since it's impossible to imagine that he's come to his senses, I have to think that maybe there's a real crisis going on there as well. And what to do about it? Mme. Ernst just came by. She's out of money to pay for her room. And I don't have anymore either. And I owe 80,000 to the tax collector, and I don't have a single penny of it. Final deadline is the end of the month. Henry was taken to the hospital. His foot looks bad. It might be the diabetes. This evening the Meysonniers arrived who are fleeing Toulon and we're going to put them up in Mémé's house. Tomorrow André Maurin arrives and we're going to let him stay here if he comes without his family. He'll take Charles's place. But if he comes with his wife and child? Where will we put them? And how to look after them? Difficult to be the only one working to support everyone. If the plays had panned out, I could have.

I'm beginning to seriously resent Lucien Jacques. It's so stupid. And I have nothing left but the deepest contempt for all those in the Contadour. Including Hélène. The phonies.

I didn't need to worry, Meyerowitz telephoned while I was at the hospital where they took Henry to clean up his foot. M. worries only about money. He's asking for money because he hired a cook!!! Yes, I'm telling the sad but absolute truth, he hired a cook. He's having a piano brought by truck to Vachères. Élise told him that I'm going to Marseille tomorrow. So M. plays the part of the desperate man, or the pariah, in which he's incomparable. But Élise is incomparable as well. I think she's the one who scores the point. Good, but the score's tied.

Henry was in a hospital ward, visibly suffering; they had operated on him an hour earlier without putting him to sleep. They still don't know what to expect. Before finding him, I looked in the smaller ward where Lucien Jacques was three years ago. Five beds holding five waxy green bodies. Hot as an incubator. Smell of pus, fishy and hot. Standing, leaning against a table, breeches unbuttoned and gaping, a kind of pale cadaver is waiting, he tells me, for the nurse to tend to him.

I hadn't finished writing that before M. called for the second time. I was fairly sure that Élise's resistance wouldn't hold him for long (Élise who has no equal when it comes to protecting herself and me). I don't answer the telephone. Aline answers and tells him I'm still at the hospital. I listen in. M. wants money (for the cook), and for me to get busy right away on *Le Bout de la route*, which he wants to make into an opera.

*December 13*

I took the seven o'clock train for Marseille. I happened to find a seat in the second class. It was terrible weather and I left the house in the dark, in the rain, so I had to use the flashlight for the shortcut by the canal. The whole compartment was talking about the attacks. Everyone wanted to have the best story. Each topped the last. If all those people had really been shot, there would be no one left in the county. Who can relate the most atrocious revenge by the Germans? Who claims to have the most heroic Robin Hoods in their forests? Who boasts of the greatest number of bastards killed in their area? Then two young women from Gap opened their bag and started attacking their provisions: sausage, roasted rabbit, fruit, cheese, wine straight from the bottle. After Pertuis, the one sitting across from me fell asleep, mouth half open, snoring, the most beautiful image of cretinism imaginable. In Marseille it was raining. It took us twenty minutes just to enter the station. Hôtel Astoria sent me to Hôtel de Paris. At noon I went to eat near La Plaine at the little place with the pregnant woman. She's getting bigger and bigger. A good meal, then I went to my meeting. Immediately I could sense that there was serious disagreement. It dragged on until about seven o'clock. Not a good day. The next day I saw L. I had lunch and dinner at his house. In the afternoon, a film, *Le Baron fantôme*, Cocteau. Beautiful images. Literary text. Dialogue with all the same flaws as mine. Not to be imitated. But a better day. A little peace and quiet. I returned late by the last tram. They were nice to me at the hotel. In the morning they served me outstanding tea. A meeting that day at eleven o'clock with Gaston Pelous. I found him demoralized, tired, and anxious. He confessed to me that he just gets by one day to the next. He asked me if I couldn't help him out. Yes, my old friend, there are tears in my eyes. That's what we're here for. Five thousand francs will be enough for him. With all my heart I'd like to do better. But I have almost nothing left. At three o'clock I went to the station to catch my train. The whole way home in the dark, I worked out the numbers and if I keep all my promises, 10,000 francs is all I'll have left. And I must pay 60,000 in January. The next day I immediately sent G. P. the 5,000. Truly I can't do more and this will cost me clothing and travel. I can't leave Manosque again unless I can get a bit more of an advance. I have to finish *Virgile* as quickly as possible, and *Deux cavaliers*. On Saturday, Salomé brought me eleven letters from neighbors at Margotte who were ordered by the provisions office to deliver supplies of potatoes that they don't have and can't get. On Sunday I wrote a letter that I sent to the director of the R.G., the prefect, and the sub-prefect of Forcalquier.

I'm getting back to work. Two good pages yesterday, two good pages today. If only I could finish by Christmas. Wrote to Cocéa to ask her permission to publish *Le Voyage en calèche*, and wrote to Gallimard to ask him if he couldn't give me an advance for this text. Frank note to Garganoff.

*December 14*

I went to the hospital to see Henry. He seems to be doing better. But yesterday he was still in terrible pain. Last evening Mme. M. arrived from Toulon at the end of her strength. Had to give her Aline's bed for now because Crébely is in my office and we can't have her sleeping in the room that C. has to go through on the way in and out. Since Aline's room is only separated from ours by a curtain in the doorway, at first I was very uncomfortable going to sleep, and then I didn't sleep well because Mme. M. was snoring so loudly. Because she was so tired, no doubt.

I'm going to try to sell a manuscript. The one for *Que ma joie demeure*. Caby came from Nice to discuss it and I proposed it to the younger Gallimard.

Mme. Ernst came by in tears. She's out of money to pay for her room. I gave her 400 francs. M. telephoned, he wants *Le Bout de la route* for an opera. He wants me to drop everything and work on *his opera*.

*December 15*

I'm rereading *Gone with the Wind*. The women are cardboard cutouts. How do they have children? With what and by doing what? Does Scarlett even have sex organs? Puppets. But the battle scenes around Atlanta are beautiful and alive. Wooden figures in the midst of all that life. Respectability. It makes you wish Scarlett would sleep with someone. A little passion, flesh, less wood, it gets annoying. Isn't there a little room in Atlanta where Scarlett could undress and make love with someone? Let her finally, somehow, be truly joined by blood to someone who experiences her breasts, her thighs, and her moans when she makes love. Let her open her thighs for once and let a man lie between them. Then the book will come to life. She will come to life. Too many veils of modesty. And how free Margaret Mitchell is with wounds. There, she says, finally, there's something I'm allowed to describe. So let her write *War and Peace*. But, as things stand, we must have Scarlett's flesh. She doesn't have the little Princess's downy mustache, and with all her crinoline, she hasn't managed to make her skirts balloon like Tolstoy's heroine as she dances in the deserted hall, coming to life. Once that happens, Mme. Mitchell, we don't need Tolstoy's women to make love. But we must have that balloon.

*December 19*

Six o'clock, and I'm writing. Three loud explosions outside at intervals of thirty seconds. The railway being bombed? Or the Sainte-Tulle factory? The electricity goes out for a moment, then comes back on. Angele who spent the afternoon with my mother and had just left, turns around, rings the bell, comes back in and says she's afraid. Élise comes up to ask me what I think of it. Nothing. And besides, it's over, all we can do is wait, we'll find out what it was. They might have attacked the pylons where the electric lines cross the Durance. I open the window. Outside, nothing. The train is arriving at the station. The Saint-Sauveur bells are ringing.

Throughout the second reading of Margaret Mitchell's long novel, one is often bored, and occasionally bowled over. The characters aren't alive. The fires are alive. Scarlett has no ass. Even when Mme. Mitchell tries to inflate her. Rhett has no balls even when he sleeps with the little redheaded whore. Property and puritanism. If Scarlett's afraid of being raped, it's no different from her fear of a toothache. A sexless novel. A drama for the castrated choirs of the Sistine Chapel. There's ten times more sex in *Le Père Goriot*, and next to Mme. Mitchell, Stendhal, that prude Stendhal, becomes a pornographer.

Gave 400 francs to Mme. E. this morning to pay for her room. Always the same financial troubles.

*December 20*

*Gone with the Wind.* Part two, finally Ashley wants to make love with Scarlett and tells her so. He even talks about making love to her outside in the mud. Finally Scarlett gets ready to prostitute herself to Rhett. Finally her heart throbs in her breast. But it's too late. She can't suddenly just come to life, she was never born. It doesn't seem authentic.

*December 21*

This morning when the cleaning woman arrived, she told us that Christiani was killed in Sainte-Tulle last evening. First we'd heard that he was the one who had killed his assailant. Christiani was a venal, mediocre man, it seems (I'm only repeating what I've heard, I didn't know him myself, not even by sight). Nevertheless he remained in the ranks after the first attack, so he was brave. He had a small construction business.

*December 23*

May God rid all our countries of patriots. No idea will ever do as much harm as the idea of the fatherland. Men are so naturally bad that after two thousand years of Christianity all it takes is a little anarchy for them to revert to the wild dogs they are. Not lions or wolves, nothing noble, but vile dogs.

Meyerowitz is in Marseille, I believe, and so I have some

peace ever since I had Aline answer the phone and tell him I was traveling.

This morning Christiani was buried amid a great showing by the militia. This afternoon Michel Auguste came by to rant and rave about the dead man. Why do people always want to put down their enemies and not acknowledge their qualities of courage or loyalty? Don't they understand they're actually putting themselves down? I didn't know Christiani, not even by sight, and I know that as a member and officer of the militia he was my enemy, but I call him courageous for going from Peyrolle to Manosque alone at night by bicycle, despite the risk of attack.

*December 24*

I have to learn some words. Enrich my vocabulary. My sentences will be more graceful and accurate. New tones will give me license, add new colors to my thoughts. Because I can always invent and construct with originality, prolifically, and tirelessly. But my sentences are poor and weak. My senses are extraordinary; I hear and I see with new ears and eyes. But the tools I use to express myself aren't sharp enough. I must learn some words. Read and pay attention to all the words that are new to me and note them down, humbly keep lists. And then have the wisdom not to use them, almost never, except a few, very rarely, so that they don't become a habit for me. Clearly prone to quiet meditation, I will always be awkward in the world. If I've lost my friends, it's from wanting to enjoy their company. They should have enjoyed my company without getting mixed up with me.

While he was ranting, A. Michel said, "He kept his nose to the ground like a dog." (Christiani was found dead in the fields near the road, in fact, his nose to the ground.)

*December 25, Christmas*

This is not a journal. It's simply a tool of the trade. My life is not completely depicted. Nor would I want it to be. As I've said, here I practice scales, I break up my sentences, I try to stick as closely as possible to the truth. But sometimes events are so rich with drama or pathos (the business with Charles) that practicing scales – my scales – isn't sufficient and I have to invent. For me, anyway, expressing truths of this order is impossible without inventing. Moreover, it's to be able to express them simply that I force myself to do this daily work. Maybe it will help me improve my skills in the direction I'd like. I was just interrupted. Mme.

Castel, the cleaning woman, was knocking on my door. I told her to come in. A formality because she's completely deaf and nearly blind. Infirmities that originated with syphilis. Ten years ago she unabashedly shared the doctor's diagnosis. She's been with us for sixteen years. Today we invited her to have Christmas dinner with us. She ate at the family table. It was very beautiful, a beauty that no one noticed. I would have liked Aline to notice. Is she too young despite her seventeen years, or too rich? Twelve people at the table, including Barbara the maid, Mme. Castel, Charles who came out of hiding, Élise's cousin André from the concentration camp (a brave fellow but mediocre, a braggart with a Tarascon temper), Aunt Noémie, a distant cousin of Élise, the widow of a family friend. Élise's mother, my mother, Élise, Mme. Henry (Henry is still in the hospital; after much worry, he is, for the moment, out of danger), me, Aline, Sylvie. That was the table. A good Christmas dinner: rabbit galantine, veal sauce, a beautiful roast turkey, chocolate cake, a very good rosé wine the color of red currants, a little bubbly (from Margotte) and coffee. With rare lack of concern for vulgarity, André drank nonstop. I don't blame him: he just spent three years in a concentration camp for Communism, and he's not even a Communist. He's lazy and sleeps like a log. He says (among other things) that he's a nonconformist. That is to say, the worst kind of conformist. He'd be very surprised to learn that I'm the true revolutionary here with all my efforts that go against the current (counter to the general opinion, against terrorism, smug Anglomania, restored Germany, the war, etc.). Charles didn't say a word. Sometimes he looked my way with a subtle, more affectionate smile than when he stayed with us before this business. Élise went to a lot of trouble for this dinner. And it was her idea to invite Mme. Castel. Élise is very good, very forthright in the best way. A small, solid, and honest woman. It's good to have her beside me. I'm often unfair to her. But even when I'm angry, when it comes to Élise, I always know that I'm being unfair, and that I couldn't ask for more than what she is and what she gives. I try hard not to get angry, but this morning Aline provoked me. I blame myself for losing control, but sapped by this pain my foot's been causing me for the last week, I let myself go. Nevertheless, it was Christmas morning and Aline's and Sylvie's shoes were here in my office, before the fireplace. I had piled them high with toys and books. That was the start of it. And Aline's unyielding, inflexible nature that gives her a severity I worry about. I love this first daughter, born in the time of our trials, who is the expression of the love between Élise and me. And who resembles me so much and is so close to me. My mistake, I believe, is wanting her to have that restraint I've gradually and painfully imposed upon myself, but only after forty-plus years and still not completely. She was awake early this morning, as I was after spending the night with an aching foot. I didn't get up right away. My foot still hurt and I was putting off getting dressed and going up to discover the shoes with Aline and Sylvie. Moreover, Charles had spent the night on the divan in my office and he wasn't up yet. I heard him stirring. I told Aline to wait for Charles to get up. Very obediently she agreed. (Had to break off here. Sick to my stomach with La Nausée. A result of all this colchicine I'm foolishly taking to reduce my pain.) So she was good and didn't let her impatience get the better of her, and I was wrong to let my pain get the better of me. But meanwhile Sylvie slipped upstairs alone. I heard the slap of bare feet. She just took one look and ran back down, and (although outraged that she overstepped her traditional rights) I was wrong to say, "That little monster Sylvie has already gone up." Aline suddenly explodes. Violence, tears, her pigheadedness, and innocent Sylvie comes into the room and looks at us dumbfounded. She didn't think she'd done anything. And Christmas was ruined and Sylvie went to collect her presents while I raged, then lectured (very calmly, but a moment later I spoiled everything again with an outburst), roared, and upset everyone. Fierce, bad tempered, shaky, I didn't want – and I didn't want Aline – to ruin Christmas. Heroically she left her presents upstairs without even peeking at them. Finally *yielding to the reasons I gave* (and not because of the presents), Aline came to me quietly about ten o'clock, apologized, and gave me a hug. She spent the rest of the day thanking me. This morning my mother came up to spend a few moments with me. She's getting old. And at noon, at the table, I had to scold her (if she knew how painful that is for me!). She picked a fight with Aunt Noémie (who is a bit like André). After lunch, I went over to kiss my mother and whispered in her ear, "I blamed you because it's your home and in one's own home, one doesn't speak to people as you did." "Well," she said with a wave toward Aunt Noémie, "she's not people."

Mme. Castel came to tell me about her husband, who's in the hospital. She had just been there. She found him much changed (I think he's going to die). She came in search of some hope, asking what I thought. I don't know, I haven't seen her husband for a long time. I shout at her at the top of my lungs that I'll go see him as soon as I can walk. "And if misfortune strikes," she says in her small deaf voice. I shout at the top of my lungs that we'll take her in, she doesn't need to worry. She squeezes my hand. She says to me, "What would I do without you, without all of you. I often think that. You are all so good." I make a dismissive gesture as though to say, "Well, yes, what of it?"

Alice Cocéa did a kind deed that I find moving. Aware of my financial worries through my efforts to publish *Le Voyage en calèche* before it's performed on stage, she sent me an advance of 25,000 francs.

To forget my pain, yesterday and this morning I quickly reread Louis Chadourne's *Le Maître du navire*... or the art of beating around the bush.


*December 29*

First, I've been quite sick with extreme pain. I'll say more about that later. Then, some serious turns of events. I'll say more about that later, too.

# 1944

*January 1*

I must learn some tricks for entering events here. The point of practicing these daily scales is to discover new tricks. Entries on Charles, on Lucien Jacques, on vast countries, woods, the green tent, Robin Hood and his Merry Men.

I just gave Mlle. Servin's sister the manuscripts for *Que ma joie demeure* and *Chant du monde*. She's leaving for Paris tomorrow morning and will deliver them to Gallimard. The bookseller is buying them for a firm 40,000 each and I absolutely need this money to pay my taxes. I'm mad at myself for all my generosities that now force me to part with these manuscripts, which I love and intended for my daughters. I'm mad at myself for being too weak to force Salomé to sell the horse (weak, but mostly incompetent). I'm not exaggerating the value of these objects. I'm being well paid for the manuscripts, but my regret lies in their sentimental value, there's not a bit of pride in it. Well, there's nothing to be done but write others.


*January 2*

Not a single problem is ever resolved; new problems just replace old ones.

Jacqueline Dez, Hélène's daughter, came to see me. Her brother, who was arrested in Grenoble by the German police, is surely going to be shot, she tells me. Young Alain is really the biggest imbecile I've ever met. I ask what he's done. The look of a heroine! Oh how carefully rehearsed it all is. She plays the hero's sister with such relish. I say, "Poor Hélène!" She says, "Oh yes, poor Maman," but she's careful to keep "the dignity of the martyr" in her speech. Although to myself I'm thinking, just a band of deadbeats, Alain, you and your sister, little tramps and good-for-nothings, without character or value. Stupid lout who finally found a label for his villainy: patriotism. That's exactly what all this drama is. She says to me, "Ah, when young men 'go to battle'!" Well, it's a two-way game, so when you come moaning that Germans "go to battle," what are you complaining about?" And if Hélène were here, I would tell her that as a pacifist who renounced her pacifism, she has nothing to say. Her son is *making war*. I warned them all that governments always find a way to introduce war and make sure it's waged. This is one of them. If Alain is shot, he will die in the war. All he had to do was not make it. The only ones who live are those who don't make war, any war. But I immediately give Jacqueline a glowing letter for A. de Chateaubriant (which compromises me) and another for Montherlant (in which I make myself perfectly ridiculous); and I ask idiotic favors from my friends. And I know that all this will come back to slap me in the face. And I do it for these vain, *soulless,* wretched beings. These destroyers of peace and of worlds, these poor excuses for suffragettes.

My health is not improving very quickly. My foot still gives me pain.

Fluchère's visit a few days ago. I was shamefully and woefully mistaken about him, and out of shame I must leave intact that entry I wrote some months back. He is loyal and loving. And most of all, exceptionally intelligent. He spoke with passion (plural, many passions, lit and burning from all sides) on the problem of Death and Justice, Aeschylus, the Oresteia, Seneca, and Machiavelli, with whom a new morality begins. Spoke to him of Luther's tract, *De Servo Arbitrio*, which he didn't know and which is relevant to his research. He left, too soon, but Jacqueline Dez was waiting downstairs. I don't see enough of him.

This evening Jacqueline ate with us, at Élise's invitation. Edith Berger was also there, having come from Lalley to discuss with me plans for publishing a book of mine that she would illustrate. I proposed to her a deluxe edition of *Vraies richesses* and *Triomphe de la vie* combined. Edith, who is and continues to be a self-made woman, has learned to express herself with great skill. It's hard to find finer qualities. Everything this woman accomplishes in all areas is admirable. Living alone now in the mountains, employed as town clerk for 250 francs a month, having witnessed her best plans quashed by a lout of a husband and the death of a child who was wanted and heroically conceived, the sole breadwinner for her mother, her sisters, and their many children (nine people), she feeds them all, *supports herself*, and paints and draws wonderfully, nonstop. I met her here in 1929 as the nursemaid who did everything for the Atgers at the Aurabelle estate. "It was you who, without saying anything, encouraged me," she tells me. (She said that better than I just did, she didn't say "encourage." I think she said "determined my course.")

Charles spoke to me about Lucien. But I'm waiting to write it down. In any case, I may have been wrong about Lucien, I ought to take the first step. I'm not a saint or angel, I don't want to take the first step. And that's wrong of me. It's not our friendship I need to write about, but the comic events that could have turned tragic. He thought of sending Charles to me. I understand very well that everything I've written is quite vague, but that's on purpose. Imagine first, morning, high up in the Boyers hamlet, the isolated house, Lucien's room with its horrible chaos of dirty laundry and watercolor paints, dirty dishes growing moldy beards, mixed with glasses for brushes, pots of Chinese ink, pans of old soup, typescript pages on the floor beside old shoes, all of it beyond description. Our Lucien is sitting on the bed, typewriter on his lap, typing out a poem, on a chair next to him a rhyming dictionary. A knock at the door, or rather no knock, three men enter suddenly, maybe four.

*January 3*

Visit from Rabi this morning, he's returning to the Krivines's after having just taken his wife and daughter to the station. Rabi is writing a play about Judas. "I want to write for the duration," he tells me. We discuss style. "Oh you," he says, "you're a master." He knows very well that annoys me, means nothing, and further-more, it's not true, I'm not a master. Rabi is very intelligent. He lives and he laughs. He giggles a bit. From one side of his mouth, as though taking a bite. I inquire about his work with much *genuine* concern. He asks me what I think of the Jewish problem. He would like me to write on the Jewish problem. He would like me to take a position. I tell him that I don't give a damn, I'm about as interested in the Jews as I am my ass; there are better things to do on this earth than worry about the Jews. What narcissism! There's nothing to do on this earth but look after Jews? No. I'm busy with other things.

So, back to our Lucien Jacques, and those three or four, hearing the clattering of the typewriter before they entered, must have thought to themselves that this time they'd stumbled on staff headquarters! The producer of incendiary tracts, the issuer of watchwords, the maker of lists. What do I know? One can only imagine what they might have imagined, in this lost hamlet of Boyers hearing that typewriter. And no, it was a poem! But they don't want to give up so easily. They're from a country without absurdity. And they must have spent long hours grilling him, not believing in the poem or the paintings or the artist. What do you do? Where does your money come from? How could they believe Lucien to be a great poet and a great painter? There was the chaos and filth, and our Lucien perhaps unshaved, for who knows how long. Their idea of the man of letters living in Paris or Berlin. And nevertheless, gentlemen, it's true, you are simply in the presence of a great and free artist and he is far removed from all the petty tricks that concern you and that seem to you huge, important things. He is another sort. Of course they laugh when he tells them simply what I just wrote, and they wonder to themselves if it could be true. He is simply an artist, gentlemen. But however much they laugh, ridicule, persist in their cruelty, sarcastically, ironically, they never stop wondering if they themselves aren't the butt of the joke. The funniest part is that they're not. At least not in the way they imagine.

*January 5*

I received an ambiguous letter from Rabi. They don't love me. They love profit. But from now on it's going to be very difficult for them to catch me in their trap. They've all been telling the most terrible lie for the longest time, a lie against the spirit. They've played all the dramatic roles: grandeur, pacifism, friendship, faith. But they themselves have remained just as their souls or lack of souls made them. Yes, the Contadour was something very important, but only for me. I had five hundred professors and I was the only student. They gave me a complete course on the absence of grandeur in men. What I learned I will never forget. Not Robert Berthoumieu, not Hélène, no one. The only man among them was Lucien Jacques. His failings still let grandeur shine through. For the others, I will never have words strong enough to condemn them as they deserve.

*January 6*

Eight days ago I wrote in *Virgile*: "With the war of 1914, the socialist Babels came crashing down." Today I read the following sentence in *The Brothers Karamozov*: "For socialism is not only the labor question or that of the fourth estate, but first of all the question of atheism, of the modern embodiment of atheism, the question of the Tower of Babel built precisely without God, not to go from heaven to earth but to bring heaven down to earth."

*January 7*

Only today have the pains abated and I can walk without limping and almost without suffering. But after a miserable night I'm too tired today to do good *invented* work, and I've written only a few lines. In the past few days, the lines for the first scene of a play have come to me, but I don't know its location or time period. There's just the hall of a castle, a captain, soldiers, chaos; they've just come from battle. The captain says to clear the hall of bodies and to post watch by the sea to report the approach of the boat. A door opens, a young woman enters. She must be thin and *white*. She asks who's in charge. The captain answers: I am. She wants to see the bodies. She seems to do this with pleasure. This may seem surprising, but she's watched her world be capsized and shipwrecked and she's concluded that if that's possible, then there's no god and nothing is forbidden. She has just discovered the enormous sweetness of cruelty. From there, it will have to develop with no preconceived plan. Led by the characters and not at all by the idea. Create them, bring them to life, leave them to their own devices as superbly as possible, and be the historiographer.

Hélène Laguerre wrote to me from Paris to ask for money. I won't give it to her. I don't have any. I need to sell two manuscripts to make some. But if I had any, I wouldn't give it to her.


*January 8*

Princess B. – You're a stranger to the castle? – No. That's my father, my mother, those are my brothers whom you have laid out as corpses in the hall that you want cleared. – And they are the ones you want to see? – Of course, what interest would I have in seeing other bodies? – I understand and I bow to you, Mademoiselle. I am not a brute. – No, of course not, I simply want to see the dead."

*January 11*

I'm rereading *La Mousson* (*The Rains Came*) by Louis Bromfield. Unlike *Gone with the Wind*, which I recently subjected to the same test, this one is a great book. The Major's appearance by Miss MacDaid's hospital bed after the catastrophe, when the old nurse revives the dying woman by talking in her ear, is a very noble human moment. Everything is right. And here's a book that includes sex, effortlessly. Noble and grand. Maybe too clever overall, maybe superficial, but that's a question for future centuries. For the moment, I'm pleased that someone has written it.

*January 19*

This morning Castel, the cleaning woman's husband, was buried. Yesterday Aunt Noémie (Élise's cousin) was taken to the hospital and this morning the surgeon didn't operate on her. He said that there's cancer throughout her stomach, and she won't live for more than a couple days. She was with us for Christmas and New Year's Day, eating, laughing, singing. This afternoon, D. came from Céreste. I hadn't seen him since his wife went mad. He told me how it happened. Sexual trauma. The story of how the Ch. family took advantage of her, how the mother, whose son is a lazy dolt, a virgin at twenty-three, stupid from masturbating, urged him to sleep with the poor woman so at least he would know how to make love. Everything about this story is both revolting and Homeric, or rather Aeschylesque. The mad woman going on and on about artificial insemination. The mother saying, "she's good for the taking," then making the son sleep in Mme. D.'s room (she's lovely, young (22 or 23), blond, melancholic, very blue eyes, full lips, petite with plump breasts and bum), and Mme. D. saying to the boy, "Come sleep with me, get naked, I'll show you how D. makes love." It was D. who told me all this. She had simply told him the whole story when she came home. She had become horribly impure, he told me. When he first arrived and I asked what was new, he broke down in tears. As he told me the story, he was no longer crying.

Élise is sick with the flu. Sylvie is sick with a cough. My mother is coughing as well. But I'm feeling better.

*January 20*

I've just finished *Virgile*. In the hospital, Noémie continues to laugh, make jokes, call desperately for food. She has no fever, she's bright, cheerful, she sings to herself in bed. Strange sort of cancer, in my opinion. I don't know what comes next, of course, but for the moment, it's better than Molière. The morose little surgeon, sullen, full of dire prognoses, circling the bed where Aunt Noémie sits enthroned, a song on her lips. Of course her sons, daughters-in-law, and grandsons also gather around her bed, not daring to say a word and gazing at one another dumbfounded!

The gendarmes are looking for Meyerowitz everywhere and this threatens everyone's safety. M. supposedly said to Mme. Ernst, "After the war, it's our turn to save Giono." Save him from what?

My sick ones are better.

Lucien phoned to invite me to his housewarming. I turned him down. Wrote a very harsh letter to Hélène. I'm absolutely determined to reject everyone. I'm breaking free, they've taken things too far.

Mme. Castel came earlier. Widow Castel. She's so deaf that even when you shout into her ear, she can't hear it. She has no money to pay for the coffin and the burial. I gave her 700 francs.

She kept asking me questions and complaining and to make her understand what I was saying I wrote it down for her in big letters on a page in my notebook. Then she covered her bad eye and looked with her good eye. Afterward, she kissed me shyly on the neck, not daring to kiss my cheek. She left a little happier.

I have a base nature. I say this because of the business with the two Lyonnais from Sainte-Roustagne. I do what must be done, I resolve not to talk about it (if I were a good soul, this would come so naturally that I'd feel no desire to talk about it.) But I do want to talk about it. That's pretty low. Couldn't being completely genuine serve as a kind of self-defense against my legend? In any case and no matter what, I'm not genuine enough to do good and keep quiet. Or if I don't talk about it, I'm so pleased with myself. Like here, for example, I can hardly keep my mouth shut, and isn't all this talk about my sincerity just a (small) roundabout way of talking about it?

What a farce this has become! We were just visiting Aunt Noémie in the hospital. Now she has peritonitis. The surgeon said, "She's going to suffer terribly. She isn't suffering, but you'll see." The nurse came with her syringe of morphine. Refusing the syringe, Noémie was bright, rosy, laughing with everyone, singing. She said, "I don't like needles. I want to eat, I want bouillon." Tired of resisting, they told themselves, "Well, she'll see, we'll give her bouillon and just see what will happen!" In fact, she drank it, smiling, fresh as a rose, then gently and peacefully fell asleep for a little nap. Vexed, the surgeon crept off, predicting in front of everyone the most rapid, ignominious death and the most atrocious agony.

Just as I predicted. I received Meyerowitz's letter, the one I've been expecting since he left. Letter full of sugarcoated threats and saccharine insults. And all this time I've been trying to salvage what he has jeopardized. (Did I ask him to make an opera out of *Le Bout de la route*? He wouldn't drop it until I finally said, "Okay, do it." But he took that "do it" to mean I was going to do it.)

*January 22*

Yesterday there was aerial combat over Manosque. The town was strewn with machine gun cartridges. A German plane was brought down and fell six kilometers this side of Pierrevert. There were six German fighter planes against a squadron of 100 to 150 English bombers. I was on my bicycle and had just passed Bois d'Asson when the noise made me look up and I saw the enormous squadron. At first they looked exactly like wild geese.

Received an urgent letter from Hélène whom I can't seem to escape. But how I despise that whole band, now.

A visit last evening from Mlle. Laugier on the subject of Martel from Banon. Perhaps I will be able to do something. Her visit to P. in Marseille yielded some results.

*January 23*

We talk about famous friends. There's Montaigne – Boethius, Castor and Pollux, Achilles and Patroclus. And now let's add Laurel and Hardy, Rivoire and Carret.

*January 27*

It turns out Aunt Noémie has an intestinal occlusion. It's the surgeon who claims this and immediately he performs a colostomy. And now there she is with this business! This woman who never suffered, remained fresh as a daisy, laughing and chatting the whole time. First she had so-called cancer, big as anything (his two arms couldn't stretch wide enough to show how big it was), then she had peritonitis (she didn't stop laughing and making jokes), but now, whether she wanted it or not, she has had a colostomy. She reeks unbearably. And amid this stench, she keeps laughing and chatting and, touching her index finger to her thumb with what she considers infinite delicacy, she says, "Now I know what I had; I had an intestinal eclosion."

But it's no longer a laughing matter. This morning Mme. Julien, her husband's daughter, arrived. She was informed by the bursar that the surgeon no longer wanted to keep Aunt at the hospital. He claims that the surgery is complete. That's a joke. What I think: he doesn't want her there anymore because everyday he has to live with his remorse. And also because now she has a terrible infection. I say to Mme. Julien that Aunt Noémie, with all her wealth, could pay for a private hospital room. She can do that. She only has to spend her money. None of her children can take her in and care for her. Why should she scrimp for them? Mme. Julien agrees with me. But the real mystery is this sick woman's good humor and serenity. There was something funny going on there, no doubt about it, but the fact remains that now there she is with her colostomy.

Fighting in Banon between inhabitants and the Gestapo, and among inhabitants themselves who – just as I had predicted – are paying each other back for all the old neighborhood quarrels over property lines, malicious gossip. They couldn't care less about the county. There's talk of machine gun exchanges, but I don't believe it. They say that Mile de Dauban was shot, tortured, and killed, Mile du Calavon says. I can hardly believe it. But a few days ago, a truck full of resisters with machine guns killed two Gestapo agents in a car on the road to Céreste, near the Lesbros farm, it seems. I heard that Gestapo agents are here as well. The same person told me he had to flee for fear of their machine guns. In any case, the air is not breathable and they evacuated Marseille. We're in for bad times.

I received the proofs for *La Terre du voleur* for which I'm writing a preface. This novel has captivated me from the start. It's beautiful and that doesn't muddle its intelligence about the human condition as our poor French writers do and will do more and more, tagging after Malraux who leaves them dumbstruck as a hen that's found a knife. I read this in a Swiss review of Malraux's latest novel: "Many readers are afraid of the abstractions that punctuate one of the chapters in this novel. It's a matter of a long discussion on the 'permanence and metamorphoses of man.' Such pages are difficult, no doubt about it," (says the critic Charles Guyot in *Formes et couleurs*, no. 4 – 1943) "but to reproach the author for them or even to assert that they are excessive and weigh down Malraux's beautiful book is to misunderstand the meaning of this work." Which means, first of all, that Charles Guyot likes showing off, and secondly, that Malraux who is super intelligent has gotten himself all tangled up in his intelligence like a silkworm in its cocoon. Oh, they are really digging France's grave. First they do a colostomy on her – so that she truly reeks and no one will miss her.

*January 28*

Our Communist revolutionaries are also aesthetes, although they'll join the fight if necessary (Malraux in Spain); fighting is part of their aesthetic. They have intelligence but not conviction. Malraux is erotic, and Aragon? Surely something, considering Gide's fear of him. If they ever gain power, I think it'll be like watching the Marquis de Sade in action. Sadism and heroism share the same root. Both are superficial distractions. But if you told that to a brave comrade (my cousin André, for example), he'd go wide-eyed as a cat pissing in hot coals. If he understood, that is. And by definition, comrades never understand.

*February 10*

My mother came up to have her nails cut. I could hear the tapping of her cane in Barbara's room. I opened the door and said, "Come in, my dear." She came in and sat down by my fire. For her it's a holiday. The whole time we're cutting nails, she and I, we're acting out a little drama. I pretend to be a brute who's hurting her and she squeals as if I were cutting off her fingers. Now she's resting. She asks me, "What is a submachine gun?" "At your age!" I say, "Why do you need to know what a submachine gun is?" "Well," she says, "I hear everyone talking about them. Is it like a rifle?" Then she understands that I'm writing and falls silent.

Wind squalls. Sky heavy with charcoal clouds. Red glow to the south. There was snow this morning. The aftermath of the storm I was caught in at Rozans the other morning.

Letter from Montherlant regarding Hélène Laguerre's son. He's doing what he can, but it isn't much. Like me. On the other hand, I can't help finding them ridiculous, the ones who now want to bend the rules of the game in question. Of course I know it could be a matter of life and death of this young man, but while he was playing he didn't care about the deaths of others. It's only now that it's his own death that he wants the rules changed. Every one of those patriots is dishonest, especially those who began as pacifists.

Montclin has been released. And I'm trying my best to get Martel of Banon released as well. He was arrested by the Gestapo. But if he did anything, it was out of foolishness or a fit of generosity and good-heartedness. Moreover, those in Banon who were really in charge, and aware, the doctor and one other (this is from hearsay), have been released and are refusing to do anything for their retained comrades. A fine display of cowardice. It's easy to imagine all these braggarts shitting their pants at the first sign of trouble.

I'm writing the preface for *La Terre du voleur*.

Aunt Noémie remains alive, without pain, laughing amid her stench.

War and revolution never kill the right people.

Read with great pleasure the delicious second volume of *Théâtre* by Maurice Boissard. Especially the beautiful *Chronique* that so aptly and justly attacks the bombast of Perrin, Langevin, and highbrow democrats. What a lovely demagogic weapon science is. Yes, truly, it's indisputable, the dust in your eyes is gold. It's good to see someone contradict the "scholars," even if it's over political inanities – you'd think he was contradicting Euclid or Newton. Nothing left but to fall into line.

*February 12*

I am small-minded. I never see clearly and completely all the aspects of issues presented to me. I finished the preface for *La Terre du voleur* in which I wanted to address (given limited time and space) the issue of human solitude. I forgot to mention the solution offered by God. I talked about this for ten minutes with M. Bellion, the sub-prefect; he sees clearly, he goes straight to the point and what he says is right. And once again, I see that my style is overly ornate and unclear. I'm trying, but I'm trying too hard. At best, I barely succeed. Sometimes it seems to me that I'll pull it off. Or at the very least, make some progress. And then I look at what I did and see that it's even worse than before. If I approach *Deux cavaliers* in this way, I'm going to write a beautiful book badly.

Bellion told me there was something on English radio about Gide. Apparently he started a review or weekly journal and published a very beautiful message on freedom. Has he been duped again? Is it Marty who brings us freedom? Isn't this just another version of Hitler? Where is freedom in the U.S.S.R.? How old is Gide now? I am always very *amorously* aroused by Gide's profound honesty. From this perspective, he has no equal. At the same time, I'm afraid that he is duped by his intelligence and his fear, and by his age. However, age would push him more toward conservatism. But now, isn't being conservative being English? I think that if the English win, it'll only be the first round. And how will they reunify this country, with the resistance, the L.V.F., the black markets, the prisoners, and all those who don't care?

*February 13*

Gaston came to see us today. And to see his son who's staying with us since Marseille is in the process of being evacuated. I spoke with him a bit this morning. I sense such distress, especially moral, that I no longer know what to do to help him. I try my best to help him with his material needs. He doesn't dare accept. He is good, discreet, sensitive. He would prefer to suffer silently. I insist. He finally accepts, but with such concern about repaying me!

I'm going to begin that short study on Froissart that *La Nouvelle Revue Française* asked me for. I would like to write clearly and make something valuable. I don't consider anything I've done to be valuable. Possibly *Colline* and *Pour saluer Melville*, but just barely if at all, and my long novels are failures. Even *Le Chant du monde*. Especially *Le Chant du monde*, which I can no longer feel, and *Que ma joie demeure*, which is spineless. I am forever my own harshest critic.

This evening, going with Gaston to the station, wonderful emerald greens in the fields where the wheat is coming up. Above, the gilded arabesques of the great bare plane trees. Imagined how fine it would be to be a painter and to go there every evening until I had managed to convey the sweet emotion those colors and forms produce.

Maybe by simply writing these daily notes, I'll come to impose upon myself the discipline of style without excess. I've been too captivated by the word and the sound it makes. I've written too easily for ten years. Those ten years I've lost. I only have the Froisssart piece to write before rewriting *Deux cavaliers*. Time to find it.

*February 17*

I realize that what I wrote on Virgil was a little too specialized for Corrêa. I have to remember that it must serve as an introduction for the *Bucolics*, *Georgics*, and *Aeneid*. It's good to have not wanted to copy or imitate, still that would have done nicely. And this will not do. I'm adding a short preamble of ten pages, a kind of fictionalized life of Virgil. For information I'm just drawing inspiration from the study at the beginning of the texts published by Les Belles Lettres. So what I'm writing is a little better and recaptures the tone of *Pour saluer Melville*. If I had any luck, and thus time and freedom, it would be best to start all over again. As with everything I've written, except *Colline* and *Pour saluer Melville*, and maybe *Jean le bleu*. That's ridiculous. I don't need to start all over. Only to make it better.

Isn't being a conservative now like being a Hitlerite or a Communist? And a patriot!

Suddenly this morning I'm grappling with the idea of writing a very great and sordid poem with *Fragments d'un paradis*, a great sea voyage, ship's log, and specific episodes, adventures. A catalogue full of richness and bitterness. The human condition but with the artistic forms of the Renaissance. I'm expressing very poorly all the wonder I feel about what this subject could hold. Not Bernardin de Saint-Pierre but Lautréamont; Rimbaud, Cook, Dumont d'Urville; Edgar Poe, Faulkner, the Melville of *Moby Dick*; and the incapacity for pleasure. The impotency of men. The vanity of all their means of power, of all their will for power. This has to be a great poem. The way to write this book would be to write it at the same time as *Les Grands chemins*. Nothing lies in my way now but *Deux cavaliers* and the Froissart piece. It might be good if I started *Fragments* at the same time as

*Deux cavaliers*. Yes, that's it, that will be a help to me. So, get to work immediately on the Froissart and finish it up quickly, from now until the end of the month.

*February 19*

Since last Sunday, I've been worried about Uncle's health. He went on another binge and headed out in frigid wind squalls last Friday to get drunk on wine and liquor. He returned at about two in the morning, hardly able to stand up. He knocked timidly on the kitchen door, so quietly that although I was on the alert, I didn't hear him. It was my mother who got up and let him in. I didn't think that he'd come home. My mother has a passionate love for this brother of hers. That's the right word for it. Since yesterday, a prostate attack, I'm guessing, because he refuses to see the doctor and fusses over himself like a recluse. But at the same time, he's afraid of dying, moans and complains, gets scared by a sideways fart. He came to see me in a sorry state, doubled over his painful belly and full bladder. I treated him as best I could for prostate. After two or three days, he began to piss again, but ever since, he gets up two or three times a night, goes down to the kitchen and heats up herbal tea for himself. Every morning he comes to update me on his health and to ask for advice. I think he may recover this time. As always, he's bored, he sets traps, and he's caught four thrushes, over twenty birds: tits, robins, chaffinches, and an extraordinary royal blue bird, tiny and splendid as a jewel.

A discussion at noon with Charles and André on Communism. How limited these narrow-minded beings are appalls me. No, it irritates me, and it's my fault, don't discuss things with them. In Goethe's time, one could still speak freely with a circle of friends. Friends don't exist anymore. I'm always very caustic in these discussions, and each time I feel ashamed for letting myself get carried away by intellectual passion. Only the passion of love exists. I scorn the rest.

*February 20*

In the evening after dinner, André, Charles, and I read. Geneva gave a wonderful performance of Beethoven's triple concerto for violin, cello, piano, and orchestra. It's wonderful. One can breathe; the world is set free. André covered his ears with his hands and read a book by Cami (!). And I realized that suddenly there before my eyes was the image of the people. Nothing could ever make them be otherwise. The dictatorship of André!

It would be magnificent! And nevertheless, André is intelligent, sometimes sensitive, good, generous, and he has a certain hunger for culture. In the camp he studied Spanish and mathematics (there are mathematics professors in particular that astound him, especially Lobry with his Inaudi-like wizardry.) But when he's offered freedom, he covers his ears – the terrible thing is that maybe he's right. Unless I'm more right than he is to agree to be duped, then swindled, in return for the payment of pleasures that Beethoven's powers give me.

*February 21*

I've come across something absolutely remarkable. Oh, that goes without saying. It's the complete works of Barbey d'Aurevilly in the Bernouard edition. I had it bought for me at a public sale in Marseille. It comes from the library of Gabriel Archinard whose books contain bookplates. I'm starting with *L'Ensorcelée*. The notes are fascinating, from the beginning. I haven't read anything yet. I only know Barbey d'Aurevilly's *Les Diaboliques*, which I read over thirty years ago. We shall see.

*February 22*

A man is always quite beautiful when he doesn't frighten his horse.

I've decided not to wait any longer to begin the long *Fragments d'un paradis* project. I'll start it at the same time as my rewrite of *Deux cavaliers*, as soon as I return from Marseille where I'm going tomorrow. Returning Friday morning. First I must accept the notion of length for this idea. Get used to anticipating a few years of work. The hardest thing in this case is the beginning. As soon as one has done enough so that the work has taken shape and one has the desire to perfect and complete it, length is no longer an issue. One then has – or at least I have – the necessary patience. I only need to get started. And, as encouragement to get started, there's the certainty that undertaking important work will bring me calm and equilibrium, and the self-esteem that I'm gradually losing. The mental vicissitudes that all the contradictory passions of the present moment make us go through destroy any equilibrium. I'm afraid of falling into a kind of violent, unjust, wholesale scorn and thus losing my joy and capacity for enjoyment. Nothing is more reassuring that knowing you're in the midst of a great enterprise. From a practical perspective, it's only a matter of dividing my days into two work periods spaced fairly far apart. That's easy enough. I'll need to get up at seven. We're heading into longer days. Lounging about, coffee, a pipe, splitting wood until eight. From eight until noon, work on *Deux cavaliers* and afterwards on *Grands chemins*. From noon until four o'clock, lunch, walk or work on *Fragments*. After dinner, read. That seems good. I'm writing this down so I can reproach myself with it if necessary. But I know myself; if I decide to do it, I will. Now to see if I have talent and resources enough to fill those seven hours. At the moment and still flush with enthusiasm, I believe I have enough of everything. But I know that there will be dark and desperate days. Heaven help me find beauty in one work as consolation for ugliness in the other. Well, why not! In fact once again, that seems good. There's every chance that the two enterprises will sustain one another and keep hope alive. In any case, waiting any longer will only serve to weaken and wear me out.

I dream of a good old age with the excellent Élise. More and more her qualities touch me. She is and has always been my surest and most understanding companion. She helps me more than anyone, without fanfare or embarrassment. And that hasn't always been very easy or very pleasant for her.

It's been a long time since I've said anything about Meyerowitz.

I hope that business is over. I was worried (as were all of those who helped him, the captain, the Jews in Mées, and all those he approached: Charles, the people in Vachères, etc.), so I was worried and I let him know that. Immediately, a total break, nothing, silence. There was talk of him last evening at dinner; Charles said to me, "I'll be the death of M." And since this declaration followed a long account of everything M. had done, it was greeted by everyone with joyous applause.

Sequel to another little story. Mme. Ernst came by this morning. I no longer mention everything I give. I no longer keep track – that's frightening. But the amazing part is that a week ago she told me that after her operation (which I paid for) she was in danger of losing "her youth" (she's my age, fifty, and at twenty, she must have been "only twenty" and maybe a bit of a "looker," that's it, period. So now that she's no longer twenty or a looker…). Politely I lamented her plight. "Yes," she said, "but there's a series of injections that can fix that now." I applauded. She simpered and, as though in passing, added very quickly, "Yes, but they're very expensive." I understood and said, "I won't let it be said that I was the cause of the loss of your youth. Would one thousand francs be enough?" "Oh, yes," she said and took the money. This morning she came asking for another thousand francs for the second series of injections! And with all of this, of course, I never have a penny! I have to write this down, or else I'll have the unpleasant impression of being duped.

Henry hasn't left yet (at this point Uncle calls me from his room. He's suffocating, he tells me. I go up to him. He has all the symptoms of asthma, he's chewing the air, he gasps and groans – all the terrifying gymnastics of those who are suffocating. I try to burn Legras powder in a saucer. It's like putting a poultice on a wooden leg, but after a moment or two, it seems to calm him down, and I return here. He had a similar attack the other evening). Henry hasn't left the hospital yet. The surgeon says he has gangrene. His foot continues to suppurate. Aunt Noémie continues to laugh and tell jokes, holding court in the midst of her stench. Old women come to pass the afternoons peacefully around her bed.


*February 26*


Returning from my trip to Marseille. I had a very good time there. I spent a long time in the Maupetit Bookstore warehouse on documents for *Fragments d'un paradis*. I've decided to begin work Monday afternoon. I've had an idea for something I want to try. Each evening I want to dictate *Fragments* to Mlle. Alice. It won't matter if she makes mistakes since the dictated pages will only be drafts that I'll review carefully, and in this way the evening work will be clearly distinguished from the morning work. Furthermore, the act of dictating will check my taste for words, will make me think only about action and image. Eliminate the aesthetic pleasures of handwriting as I described them in *Virgile*. Economy of means for the sake of the value of the text. I'm sure this is a good idea. In any case, the experiment excites me.

*Evening.* More and more determined. I've had special desk pads made for Alice. I've spoken to her about this new project. She didn't seem too upset. She didn't turn red as a beet and take on that pursed look she gets when her inferiority complex takes hold of her liver and spleen. More and more convinced that this experiment can and must produce wonderful results. It can be continued wherever I happen to be, with either Alice or Élise. This evening I'm waiting for the books I bought in Marseille. I'll start immediately with those that should help me develop the first chapter, launch myself right into the image and adventure, which may be very beautiful.

Just saw Mlle. Alice. She seems delighted with this new project.

Sent Louis a telegram of 150 words to boost his morale regarding his summons to the S.T.O., and at the same time I'm doing everything I can to get him out of this mess. But the most urgent thing is that he knows he's not alone or abandoned, and that people are working for him.

Despite *Fragments*, I must not abandon these daily (or almost) notes that are so useful to me.

*February 27*

The books I found in Marseille to begin *Fragments* didn't arrive last evening. Now the bus won't come again until Wednesday.

At first glance, Barbey d'Aurevilly is dazzling. After a while, only a few magnificent descriptions of women and women's flesh hold up. All the rest is only glitter. The images are mostly naïve, childish, and terribly inflated. Nevertheless some unusual words, well placed, do retain my interest. Meandering parentheticals often make sentences incomprehensible. Comparing the life in Balzac's *Les Chouans* and the poor use Barbey makes of his peasants and passions in *L'Ensorcelée*, one knows immediately what must be done and what must be avoided and why one of these two books is great. Barb. has no gift for life. Once in a while, in passing, a woman's breasts are alive and her flesh is on fire, but that's all, she has no soul, it's a beautiful iridescent snail we hunger for and want to swallow. It doesn't fill us with love as is the case with Sanseverina, about whose breasts and thighs we know nothing, moreover.

*February 29*

Last evening I dictated eight pages of *Fragments*. The first eight. The books arrived a little later. This morning I've written three pages of *Deux cavaliers*. It's going to be hard work, but I'm continuing. What was dictated is only a first draft that I'll have to do more work on. Each of these chapters must be continually reconsidered and developed afterwards. Nothing of what I dictate is definitive. For *Deux cavaliers*, after the first chapter: "The Story of the Jasons," the second will be "Raphaël." I took out the marriage of Ange (who becomes Raphaël) and I describe the youngest brother as I'm telling the story of the Jasons. Today I'm going to dictate the second chapter of *Fragments*, on *the winds*.

The business with Louis is completely straightened out.

*March 1*

Dictated ten pages of *Fragments* this evening. Obviously what I dictate isn't beautiful. It's even fairly ridiculous and most of the time affected. But I have a solid base there for constructing the work itself. The general mood will require me to find the right tone when I switch to writing. I think this is good. For *Deux cavaliers*, I see forming an idea that would have me reapplying the method of *Grands chemins*. In any case, I'm going to write the second chapter entitled "Raphaël" so as to establish the parallel between him and Marceau. I must follow the adventures of the two men. Third chapter "The Town of Lachau."

For the second chapter of *Fragments*, an episode, full of swearwords, to enter into the life of the ship's boy. His country, his mother, his sisters. How he lives. In such a way that the invention of the swearwords will be tremendous, and truly *to invent* the swearwords. (Yes, that's difficult, but look again at Lautréamont – moreover this will give depths to the gulfs of the sea and the black of the drums, but now, to write it.)

*March 1*

This chapter is very important. Beginning with this story full of swearwords, one must see the gulfs themselves deepening, from which the fragments of Paradise will arise. This is where it must take shape. It's imagined, but it isn't written.

I'm pretty satisfied all in all; nothing is definitive but everything is taking shape and getting organized. Without question, the fact of dictating requires that I keep the action moving in a magnificent way. It keeps things clean.

*March 2*

Dictated fourteen pages of *Fragments*. This will provide good material in the end. Must continue. Saw this morning that *Deux cavaliers* can become a very beautiful book. Especially the chapters that I'm going to start work on, "Raphaël" and "The Town of Lachau." There are very beautiful things in what I've already written. The order and logic of the work requires continuing to dictate undisturbed without trying to revise, until I've finished writing *Deux cavaliers* and *Les Grands chemins*. Then I'll find myself with almost 2,000 pages of incredibly rich material, ready to work with. And noting here each day or each time, the discoveries

I need to work on. That way, my notes won't be lost. I just have to glance through the notes since February 28 to find what I've decided or wanted to do.


*March 4*


Just now suddenly someone knocked on my door and in came Lucien, smiling as if he had never left. We embraced – with such deep joy on my part – and it's over, and there was never anything wrong between us, and everything is cleared up, and I am very happy.


*March 11*


One of these days I'll talk about my trip to Marseille from which I returned yesterday. The last evening, an alert, and violent reaction by the D.C.A. I got up and went down into the hotel lobby. I realized that all shelters are illusory, of course. During the previous day I saw a roundup on the square behind the Stock Exchange, where the tobacco black market openly takes place. But the presence of so many armed police everywhere is unbearable. In the evening, after dinner with Gaston P. and H., altercation with two policemen out of uniform, completely drunk, who wanted to take our taxi. In the end they humbly apologized in front of H. So much so that I was disgusted by them. At first they showed unparalleled insolence and arrogance. A sudden reversal; they were so eager to shake our hands. They were trying to win a kind of approval. They apologized, blaming the difficulty of their work. Gaston P. wasn't disdainful enough of them, but H., how haughty he was, and what pleasure it gave me.

*Sunday, March 12*

A sentence in Barbey d'Aurevilly reminds me that I've had the misfortune of not keeping my father's tools. I remember his old hammer where he left the mark of his hands. There were two spiral hollows in the handle. There were his awls and leather knives as well. All that was stupidly sold. I remember that I thought about it at the time. But I hardly guessed how precious those tools would seem to me now, and what a comfort it would be to fill those dear hollows with my own hands. I must have been very young and thoughtless to have sold such rare tools. They must have gone for ten or fifteen francs in those days. I know that my mother could never again look at "Veilladou," his work bench, low and marked at the corners where he put the wax, pitch, glue, the boar bristles for his cord, and that she sold the table with his hammer, leather knives, and awls, all the painful reminders of her tall dark husband with the white beard; "Père Jean" as he was called.

I learn from a note in *La Gerbe* that Gide gave a speech on Algerian radio. I'm sorry not to have heard it. It's one of two things: either he's a Russian prisoner and he's refuting that he's returned to Russia under duress, or else the propaganda created on this side about the Bolshevik bogeyman is false and exaggerates the Communist threat. I would be tempted to believe the second of these possibilities. For me, it's not a question of doubting Gide's honesty. Algiers might thus be true freedom. That's something to think about. Something else to think about, too, are those violent, thoughtless, drunk police who revealed their dangerous inhumanity in Marseille the other night. How does A. Gide intend to settle things with Aragon who terrified him *physically*? After so much intelligent preparation, is A. Gide going to ruin his own death? But up until now, everything has been so magnificently constructed that I have a hard time believing that. That he would see through to the end so much preparation and then compromise the result in the final moments? That doesn't seem like him. So much so that his taking a stand reassures me. What's happening could simply be a bad ending and not the bloody dawn of a new era. Or perhaps universal suffrage, parties, all talk, the *N.R.F* and commerce and the A.E.A.R. and the journal *Vendredi* and Jean Guéhenno and André Chamson, editor with Geneviève Tabouis and articles by Andrée Viollis and a good joke on the organized, conscious proletariat. A kind of "we take them and start again." When I say reassured, what I'm really saying, what I mean, is that I find confirmation here of my resolution to scorn henceforth all that bears the name of man. And that basically I'm not mistaken when I claim that all of this is just a dark comedy.

Yesterday I dictated nine pages of the Captain's journal for *Fragments* and did three pages of *Deux cavaliers*. In *Fragments*, I've reached a point where I must now begin to give it tone.

*March 13*

In Algiers, A. Gide is associated, no, is allied with Maritain. Old accomplices at heart. There's no need to wait for the revival of this band of intelligentsia that even includes the Julien Bendas. I imagine that in Paris Jean Paulhan must be preparing his game bag and at Gallimard they must be making the super-mock-up of the super-forthcoming *N.R.F* for the victory. A mix of *N.R.F* and *Commune* as in lark paté. One lark, one horse, half and half.

I see the Guéhennos already seething at the half-pay and André Chamson polishing up his Legion of Honor medal. If a return to all that is the reason for having destroyed London, Berlin, and the rest of them, I say it's a bad bargain. Well, as for me, I'm waiting for Aragon and Malraux to enter the fray. One of two possibilities here as well. Either they will enter persona grata together, rolling A. Gide slowly along in a wheelchair while Guéhenno plays ballads on the accordion and Chamson passes the hat among honorable society. Or else they'll be bulls in the china shop. In the latter case, A. Gide will die, suddenly and badly, Guéhenno will go to Sainte-Hélène, and Chamson will set up an ass-kissing factory. I don't really see what all that fanfare has to do with Art. If I succeed *in living* meanly in the midst of all that, it will remain my job to write books well here that will no longer be published. Of course Maritain will be the turkey for the first banquet. So let them be thrown out of government offices immediately, hell and damnation! Since that's what they've set their sights on. That's the only way they'll stop being such pains to their writing desks. And let someone somewhere, I don't know who, finally write *Don Quixote* and *Macbeth*.

In *Redgauntlet* by Walter Scott (who, let us not forget, wrote a satirical history of Napoleon) I read this: "It was not of late years that the English learned that their best chance of conquering their independent neighbours must be by introducing amongst them division and civil war" (it's a Scots who's speaking).

This evening I dictated seventeen pages of *Fragments* in which the Captain, M. Larréguy, and Mr. Jauréna emerge. Captain's journal. I am dictating better. My sentences are clearer. It's still a rough sketch of what I want the book to be, but there's much more good work than in the earlier pages. This morning magnificent progress on *Deux cavaliers*. Now that I know where to highlight the two brothers' love, this book is incomparably richer and cleaner than its earlier version. It's good work. I can't tell yet if the morning work helps the evening work, but the evening work certainly helps the morning work. Add taking these notes and my days are very full. Since March 1, I've dictated seventy spare pages for *Fragments* and written twenty-one full pages for *Deux cavaliers* (at least forty if dictated as above).

*March 15*

A young lieutenant commander who came to visit me and to whom I spoke about my plans for *Fragments* mentioned that it would help me to read *Instructions nautiques*. "It's precise," he told me, "and as though written by a kind of poet, so that

I've often read it for pleasure while I'm on watch. Sailors," he continued, "are always poets." Immediately I saw what good use I could make of these *Instructions nautiques*. I telephoned Gaston to have him find them for me at the Librairie de la Marine in Marseille (33 Rue de la République). There he was told that I must first obtain a form from the head of the German Maritime Transportation Office in Marseille. I immediately requested that form. If I can't get the manuals before the war ends, they'll still be of use to me afterwards for finalizing the work. It's information that shouldn't be neglected. Moreover I think I'll find deep poetic joy in simply reading these books. I want that very much.

This morning, three good pages of *Deux cavaliers* on Marceau's love. This evening, dictated fourteen pages of mysterious conversations between the Captain and M. Larréguy in *Fragments*. Just noticed while I was resting on the divan that the two works are mutually beneficial, that when I exhaust the inspiration for *Fragments*, I go to *Deux cavaliers* with ease and joy. When I write *Les Grands chemins*, it's going to be magnificent, delightful.

*March 17*

Finishing my pages this morning (three very good ones), I realized that one work is incredibly helpful to the other. When I leave *Deux cavaliers* (who truly are two Cavaliers now, and I love them, and this is going to be a beautiful book), I *want* to work on *Fragments*.

Attacks against me in *Les Lettres françaises* [clandestine Communist paper]. I have no talent and I attract a following of cowards: lecherous viper.

*March 18*

Impossible to read *Une vieille maîtresse* by Barbey d'Aurevilly. This makes five times I've had to put it down. Mme. de Mendoze, Hermangarde: I keep asking myself what Stendhal would have done with them. I couldn't finish *L'Ensorcelée*. I read *Le Chevalier des touches* and *Les Diaboliques*. *Une histoire sans nom* disgusted me and I gave up a quarter of the way through. It sent me back to Walter Scott whose *Redguantlet* and *The Pirate* I found ravishing, and whose work I intend to keep reading.

There's no book I want more than the *Instructions nautiques*.

Dictated nine pages, but without pleasure, copied from the voyage of Dumont d'Urville. Not much creativity but it's not without interest to me. It's only a starting point, there's work to be done. On the other hand, wrote three good pages of *Deux cavaliers*.

*Sunday, March 19*

"I don't like man, I like what devours him – knowing to prefer to man the eagle that feeds on him. – Nothing easier than erecting temples from the already cut stones of old buildings; but to cut fresh the stone extracted directly from the earth, that is something that cannot be done without great effort and much trial and error."

A. Gide
*Letter to Montgommery Belgion*
*November 22, 1929*

*March 24*

I've convinced the *N.R.F* to publish the translation of *Trabajos de Persiles y Sigismonda* by Cervantes. A book without which Cervantes's whole message can't be understood. Pilles will do and put his name on the translation. I've already translated *Moby Dick* with Lucien Jacques. Not to mention Joan Smith whose name is on the cover to grant her a third of the royalties. She only served as a living dictionary for us. And I have in a notebook the literal translation of Fielding's *Joseph Andrews* that I had done by a freemason, the primary school inspector who was dismissed at a time when he was full of self-doubt. I gave him this project to help him regain confidence. Camoin, Aline's English teacher, reviewed the text. So I will have succeeded in bringing into French culture the translations of three beautiful foreign works.

Work continues at the same rhythm. *Fragments* progresses by ten to fourteen dictated pages a day, that is five typed pages, and *Deux cavaliers* by three pages a day, which will easily fill seven typed pages.

Received authorization to buy *Instructions nautiques*, very easy. Now I need to find out if the Librairie de la Marine in Marseille can get it to me. I've asked them.

*Sunday, March 26*

At noon over lunch, short and sharp altercation with Aline who behaves more and more badly, never getting up, refusing to help with anything at all, never setting the table or going to answer the door. I shook her hard, she took off without finishing her meal. She still hasn't come back. A proud, stubborn nature, selfish, basically mean, uncompromising, without tenderness or real affection. Princess, determined to get her way without giving in.

*March 29*

Coincidence: list of students receiving their law degrees in Aix: Jean Jerphanion.

This morning six hundred German troops arrived, roads blocked, machine guns set up in the streets and especially at the Saunerie crossroads. Papers checked, Curet arrested, I believe (not to be confused with "curé," this is a lawyer named Curet). This was the morning that students from the high school left for Digne where they're going to take their exams. They were stuck in Saunerie and the principal had to come back to straighten things out. Aline and Guy Pelous had also left for Digne but had taken the shortcut, so they weren't stopped. At least that's what I assume, since they haven't returned. They must be in Digne by now. But

I really wish that Élise had called at the hotel where they got out. The exam is tomorrow.

Remarkable clumsiness of the Germans.

Dictated fifteen pages of *Fragments*, but not happy with the very poor quality generally of this poetry, which must be quite rich to make the book what I want to make it. Of course all that must be written and not dictated. But I was expecting higher quality from the start.

Wrote three pages of *Deux cavaliers* which is very clean up to now. What follows is more difficult.

It seems they arrested and carried off two truckloads of men and women under dubious circumstances. I've been sheltering a terrified Mme. E. all morning, and Ch. never goes out of the house anymore.

*March 30*

To the Communists. – What you want to destroy are the best (aristocratic) forces. You will protect and use someone like Maurois because he's useful despite being a bourgeois industrialist. You will destroy Poulaille, Lucien Jacques, Guilloux, and me because we aren't useful despite coming from and remaining part of the working class. But from birth we have been adversaries of attempts to debase us. Revolutionaries in the true sense. My father would never have been a Communist. Tomorrow (not today but tomorrow) the Communists here (in Manosque) will be Martin-Bret, Curet, Auguste Michel. (This would be incomprehensible to a reader who doesn't know these individuals but it's perfectly clear to me).

*March 31*

Dictated 170 pages of *Fragments* since February 28 that I'm very unhappy with. I haven't found the rhythm or the spirit. Everything is hodgepodge and drawn out. I have to make myself continue, my only hope is finding the way when I begin to write. Nevertheless, I think I must keep dictating to assemble as many pages as possible and try my best to enrich them without being surprised at not succeeding as well at this as through thoughtful writing. At the same time, wrote 56 pages of *Deux cavaliers* and those are good.

*April 1*

Rest today. I didn't want to dictate, or to write, and I didn't force myself. Going back over the 170-some pages I dictated, I realized that it was very bad. There's nothing, no true poetry, no grandeur, and especially no composition, no style. For the moment, it's very much below sub-Jules Verne. Nevertheless, I must keep dictating, even if it must remain of so little value. All the work will consist of carefully considering the form. When I've found the form – and I can find it – everything will take on body and soul. Corresponding to a new book must be a new style and construction. Finding that style, that construction. Making it (the construction) as new as the idea. Writing the dialogues. Bringing the characters to life (who aren't alive) (but I am going to do that). Finding the construction that will be able to bear the weight of the whole poetic invention and most importantly, inventing (but that is not completely the role of the dictation – its role was to let the book emerge, to rough it out, and it has perfectly fulfilled that). So, continue and from now on work on the general construction and at certain points go deeper. But as soon as I'm seized by the truth of a style and original composition I'll be swept along and everything will organize itself. So, starting Monday, back to work. On the other hand, what I've written of *Deux cavaliers* is very good.

I just saw Borrély again. A short conversation in which I found him to be just as he was and he found me to be just as I was, just as I am, without the legend. That is to say, sticking to my position, unchanged: a pacifist. Nothing more. He informed me that Martin was condemned to death by the Communists. So the wolves feed on one another. Nevertheless, from the simple perspective of the nation, if one must resist and fight, Martin acted nobly (disregarding the taint of his ambition). And so? So, remaining as I am, a foreigner to the Germans, English, Americans, and Russians. Not enemy, not friend, a foreigner, not getting mixed up with one side or the other. Borrély is the only one I've found intact. I was right to love him.

For *Fragments*. Maybe give the ocean a personality (thus redo the wind, chapter two, making it a living element of the world – see lyrical process in *Poids du ciel* but reinvent it for this particular plan). A Dionysian book *but written by Fielding*!! Gradually discovering!

Romain Rolland who is not of the working class believes in the working class; but I am of it and I do not believe in it.

Ch. Péguy
(Remark reported by Julien Benda,
N.R.F., XLIX, 1937, 210.)

*Sunday, April 2*

*For Fragments* – Maybe use the present tense for the cosmic characters, wind, squid, monsters, etc. (list blue notebook). For the wind, for the ocean, that could be beautiful.

Enrich the vocabulary of "FOREIGN" words.

Bring *the life* of the ship to life. Render it tiny through the use of cosmic characters, but make it visible that way in all its detail and variegations, as though seen through a microscope. But I insist, *very much alive*. The human characters very much alive as well.

The greatest care for style in this tennis game where the words must play with the image. Short and *very rich* sentences. Never return the ball into the box where the reader is expecting it.

That is all too thought out, and consequently will be difficult to achieve. But continue trying until it takes off.

From now on, producing a passage, or one part (the wind, for example).

The *detective novel*. The literature *of attitude* that's responsible for all the books written since Balzac (and that are bad Stendhal, Stendhal misunderstood) broke creation down into two parts: the tedious and a precipitate of the picturesque, the dishwater and the precipitate. The detective novel is a condensed version of the picturesque: *a mysterious matter* minus Balzac. All the other books are dishwater and most of the time they're enough to make you sick. On the other hand, consider Fielding. Which proves that Stendhal's message was not understood. Formula for *Fragments: a cosmic detective novel.*

That's all very fine, but it has to be done.

More on the detective comparison: instead of the story being the development of the subject (what I've done until now), *the subject must arise from the development of the story.* Paying close attention so that will perhaps shape the construction and style. *Let maximum attention be born of maximum expectation. The least object must have the greatest possible interest* (this connects with, confirms, and certifies all that I've noted above on the style of the work, the microscopic life. So at the moment my thinking is logical and coherent).

Careful! Better not to know too much about what must be done, or it all collapses like over-whipped mayonnaise. Many examples!...

Invent the inimitable signs of experience and habit. *Invent*.

Again, the detective comparison: so *a secret logic* (consequently, what's wrong with the Captain's conversations and explanations as I dictated them – moreover I felt that and that's what prompted this clarification for what will follow).


*April 3*

The immobile traveler: where I go, no one goes, no one has ever gone, no one will go. I go there alone, it's a virgin country and it disappears beneath my feet. A pure journey. Encountering no one's tracks. The country where deserts are truly deserts.

Tomorrow I'm going to Marseille to take steps toward easing the pain for Mme. Martel whose son and husband are lost in the prisons, no one knows where they are now. I asked for a letter of introduction to meet with the head of the Gestapo and I'm going to see him. I dislike this. For those who want to think badly of me, it could be seen in a bad light, and no doubt will be.

A revealing passage from Guéhenno in *Europe* from March 15, 1932 (quoted in *N.R.F.* 223 1-4-32, p. 777) on the disarmament of intellectuals. This is from the period when the U.S.S.R. was pacifist and I was a Communist sympathizer. A moving letter, the article says, but a letter that finally *dupes those it moves*.

"You are surprised that the world takes no interest in your debates. For once address an urgent and true question: the world will pay attention. *Dare to make decisive commitments* (the emphasis is mine). Then those men will hear you. Your words will sink deep into the open ground and will one day bear fruit. You want to return to the intellect its primacy and its honor. You know, Gentlemen, that it lost them to the war, *by taking part in it*, by being applied to justify it. By turning against the war, it can regain them. Whether we witness its spectacular revenge or definitive abdication all depends on you.

"If war came, what example would you set for us? Would your meeting rooms in Geneva be closed? Would each of you remain in your own country? Would you write some propaganda brochure, sign manifestos on French civilization or Germanic culture, or would you remain silent, or not? *Or, once again, would you refuse to enter into this system of violence* (again, the emphasis is mine)? *Would you say that if war has the power to kill us it does not have the power to debase us again, that it will never again possess our hearts and our will?* There is a political stance that says: As long as I am here, there will not be war. Would you have the same courage, *and for as long as war lasts, would you dare to respond that you are not here?*

"And as for us, what would we do? Those pens that Aristide Briand himself claimed were made of the same steel as canons, dear Gentlemen, could they all be ours now? Gentlemen, you know that without you, without *us*, war is impossible To lead the poor bread eaters to the trenches, to the edge of their tombs, all your discourse is needed, all *our* articles, all *our* songs. By themselves, they would not go. But we play on their instincts. We alone know how to lie well enough to make their own deaths appear beautiful to them. Fifteen years ago we were witness to this singular work. *We were disgusted enough by it to swear never to participate in it.* We promised this to ourselves. We promised it to a whole dead youth, to our friends, and *we must keep our promise*."

NO COMMENT WHATSOEVER. NONE.

Perhaps through association with the preceding idea, I'm thinking that I've said nothing more about Aunt Noémie. Ah yes, she's alive, she's alive and well, she laughs and eats. Eats, alas, because she's alive, but she stinks horribly from her colostomy that fouls her with excrement non-stop.

Attempts to push ahead on the part of the wind in *Fragments*. But with mediocre results and finally abandoned. Nothing new. Nevertheless it's clear that yesterday's efforts head in the right direction and I've found what must be done – in particular with the cosmic characters, and even in the details, yesterday's work is valuable – but I still have to find the means by which to do it. Gradually, moreover, the Fielding form takes shape for a project so far removed from Fielding: Ocean-Tom Jones, Rain-Joseph Andrews, Storm-Squire, Typhoon-Jonathan Wild, Breezes-Amelia. Similar characteristics and even processes. (I'm speaking of inner processes). The tool, that is to say, the sentence, I'm hoping to learn from *Instructions nautiques*. Because there's pepper in Henri Michaux's sentence (and sometimes his process) that can often be valuable (drawn forward sentence by sentence, dramatic intensity of the word, capstan of the image that endlessly offers one turn further), but I need a very long-winded sentence here. One can't run 3,000 meters with a 100 meter technique.

So today, once again, rest, profitable rest. (I call rest not writing, either in *Fragments* or in *Cavaliers*.) But at every moment, I reproach myself for my so-called rest.

Also: carefully merge the human characters and the element characters in an action devised by the latter and encountered by the former: Little Red Riding Hood is going to bring the cake to her grandmother but will encounter the sun coming from millions of kilometers away, and the wind perhaps coming from the Kara Sea, and thus the drama, nothing to do with the wolf.

*Wednesday, April 5*

Returned last evening from Marseille after having obtained, I believe, Martel's release. Happy to inform his wife who was waiting for me at the station. But no good news to give Mme. Curet. Marseille unbearably hot; everywhere the terrible odor of shit (no other word to use for it). Rue d'Aubagne, a big window display of roses smells like shit. The streets are full of the smell and women on the streets, made up and dressed to kill, their lungs fed on the odor of shit, stroll about, oblivious as princesses in a garden.

Meiffret wrote to me in passing that my name is on a black list. Really? I can't imagine why!

Maman is sick. Sylvie is feeling better. As for me, I've got the flu, which I caught in that pus incubator, Marseille.

*Thursday, April 6*

Oh yes, there is a reason why I'm on a black list. Aren't we entering the era of mechanization, technology, slavery, State capitalism, the abolition of the individual, a time entirely occupied, directed, and organized collectively – buying on credit, even the pen, American society, automatic dishwasher that plays syncopated Brahms or Bach as jazz, André who covers his ears and hums while they're playing Handel so that he can read Ole & Axel in peace. Industrialization of arts and leisure and love. Of course, what more reason do you need, aren't those enough? Come on!

Began dictating *Fragments* again. It's still very bad. Maybe an idea to impel a part of the work. Chapter on the wind. But I'm still not ready to write it. I'm waiting for the *Instructions nautiques*. Maybe that will give me the boost I need.

Wrote barely three sentences for *Deux cavaliers*. I don't dare touch it being so disinclined.

*Friday, April 7*

Whoever can do the most can do the least. I can be minister but I can't resole my shoes. So to be minister is the least.

A strange period. I have the feeling that everything's gone to hell, that there's nothing solid under me anymore, not work, not anything else, even what I valued most. No desire to work. Nothing in mind. *Deux cavaliers* stopped dead at the end of a sentence and it's impossible for me to continue. What I need of course – I think – is fresh air, to walk. I know what the best remedy is. Continue just the same, even if it's bad (and it will be bad), even if it's very bad, even if it means destroying what will be made that way. But what an effort it takes to "take it upon oneself." Especially since it's easier said than done. Dictated four short passages of *Fragments* and wrote nothing of *Deux cavaliers*. Where will the spark come from? I'm reading, but I'm reading old issues of *Revue de Paris*. Holy week outside. Gray days, spring, brilliant buds on the chestnut trees, wind, warm, muggy, close.


*Saturday, April 8*


It was a little over a year ago, in December 1942 in Bourges, that I saw a little boy who was crying beside his donkey who was dying on the road. It was at the far end of Bourges near the station, near the bridge over the little river. The donkey's suffering was horrific; the tears of the boy, atrocious because silent and with the horrible grimaces of the possessed. I remember I had a terrible desire to open my wallet and pay for the donkey, I don't know what, give the boy 1,000, 2,000 francs. I didn't do it. False shame stopped me. I thought to myself, what will you look like? Will that boy even understand? You're being ridiculous. I also wanted someone to kill the donkey to end its suffering. But I remember the pathetic looks the boy gave the donkey. Maybe he was crying less for his loss than for the suffering he saw. This scene just suddenly sprang to mind and I'm blaming myself harshly for not having had the courage to get beyond my fear of looking ridiculous. My lack of nobility brings me physical pain once again. I had the *opportunity* to do good and I didn't *spoil* it but *ignored* it out of absurd fear. That's unforgivable.

"It is high time that America produces the dreamers who will save it from itself."

> Duhamel
> (*Scènes de la vie future*,
> WHICH IS A GREAT BOOK.)

A book that provides the human *dimension* better than all of Malraux's books and all of Aragon's eyes.

One revolution after another like Chicago slaughterhouses.
Robespierres (plural!) with electricity and *technology*.

Something else: there is nothing but reality throughout. Thus a logic of pathos must be found for *Fragments*.

Visit from Mme. Curet asking me to intervene to have her husband released. Naturally I'm going to do everything I can, but I can't do very much. I'm going to write a letter to G. Pelous so that, through the police intendant, a meeting can be set up between Mme. Curet and some Gestapo leader in Marseille. (I'm thinking of course that it's not possible to call twice upon the kindness of the same person who helped Martel without jeopardizing the good outcome of the intervention for Martel – it's like matches: they can't be used twice.) Tomorrow I'll also go to see Pierre Aubert, the deputy mayor, so that he's part of our efforts. No matter that he's a personal enemy of Curet. Aubert is capable of grandeur. In the end, I don't know how I can do anything; I'm so unqualified and so powerless.

Seem to have returned to *Fragments*, dictated eight pages, and some ideas for *Deux cavaliers*, very good ones, will allow me to write tomorrow and to continue.

*Tuesday, April 11*

Nothing works. It's all hopeless. I mean it: hopeless.

*Europe* no. 111 – March 15, 1932. Jean Guéhenno: "Intellectuals and Disarmament":

page 323: "...Then Chamson spoke..., he evoked the war:

the dishonor of the past that could be the dishonor of the future. The time had come for a commitment *once and for all*" (the emphasis is mine because in 1939 Chamson, as captain or no less than staff officer, staff captain, let us remember, sounded the battle cry in speech, in writing, and in his swagger, wrote on heroism – *N.R.F.* 1939 – pushed for war from 1938 to 1939, and studded with medals (*crachats*! spit! the perfect word), started this squabble. The reason for the two positions – because this is no idiot, this is only a dishonest man: Orders from Moscow. If he and Guéhenno were pacifists *once and for all* in 1932, it's because Moscow *needs* pacifism for its politics (I let myself be taken in) and if in 1939 and today they are warmongers, it's because Moscow needs heroism. (As for me, I continue to be a pacifist, contemptuous of them both.) They will become ministers and I will be shot. There must always be lying and retractions. That's how one *succeeds* if one is not someone else. If one can do nothing but *succeed*). Leave the *once and for all* for the honest folks. But how to explain the *just this once* in this *once and for all*?

*Friday, April 14*

If you want to better understand the course of those who have taken "a position within Communism," you must read the pages (printed on red paper) that *Variétés* published at the beginning of its special issue: "Surrealism in 1929." There Louis Aragon and André Breton discuss the fate of Trotsky (exiled by Stalin). There you can find the phrase, "a poor man's Robespierres." There André Thirion writes: "... that crook Malraux who, let us hope, will continue his nasty-old-bastard business by offering as a sequel to *Les Conquérants* an adventurous life of Colonel Lawrence, who now passes for one of the revolutionaries. Everyone's after a 'chair of clouds' for their little asses." I'm keeping this issue of the review with my documents. Unfortunately the first five pages are missing. There you can see how to "organize the pessimism." Always the pranks of schoolboys making "a toad smoke a cigarette," so that its stomach will finally explode like a firecracker when it's inflated enough. Nowhere do I find passionate reasons for an honest man.

The work has started again. This morning wrote a page and a half, good ones, for *Deux cavaliers*. This evening dictated eleven pages of *Fragments* and this afternoon a few insights on what *Fragments* could be, if I don't kill it off by over determining the reasons and requirements for it. Or make it so beautiful that it then escapes my feeble grasp. Theory: *There are no imaginary worlds*. Everything in this book must be worked in the direction of the image. There is only the real world. Avoiding everything that could make *Fragments* seem like a utopian novel – especially philosophy and social science. Nothing by the truth, and on that subject, carefully remaking the psychology of the human characters, rendering them *very ordinary*, not exceptional in any way except in the *Conception of reality*. Bringing together physical descriptions: mustaches, ways of walking, voices and looks, and linking them to the real world through details on families, wives, relatives, sister-in-law, aunt, mother, and on the villages, countries, etc., all that can *easily* be Fielding before blending them with what will be *difficult* to make Fielding.

The revolution, the novelty, the *renaissance* must be in the *conception of reality* or a new way for man to *encounter reality* (new or *reborn*). Not in the opposition between *the real* and the *ideal*. On the contrary, the real is stranger than the ideal, *more difficult to believe*, more ideal, and that's how it should be, as it's created by forces that are more imposing and more mysteriously powerful than the ideal (fruit of simple imagination, whereas the real…).

*Fragments* must be an *intellectual revolt*.


*Saturday, April 15*

*On these notes*. This is the self-portrait of the Artist. But how to portray as well his colic, La Nausée, anger (yes, perhaps) and that small place in his heart, hidden even to himself, where even he doesn't always know what's happening? What to do with all that? Maybe one can see his blue eyes and his attitude. The pose, as slight as it may be, is a pose. He is trying to act natural, but since he's trying, it's still a pose. Pinned alive like a butterfly? But then it's going to die, though there'll be one hell of a pose to display, that butterfly with its wings spread! So, admit that this isn't everything, that in addition to the portrait he is also alive, and try to see him when he puts down his palette and brushes. To do what? Well, to live: to eat, drink, enjoy himself, be afraid, show off, lie, and thus drawing truth from the belly as though worming information out of himself.

*Tuesday, April 25*

Have since gone to Sornes, to Sigottier. Magnificently welcomed by Penzin who showed me his mill for hulling spelt and then gave us a taste of the country: ham, sausage, jam, fruit, and wine. So, in the little hollow valley where Penzin's mill sits amid primroses, and not far from the blue rocks of Sigottier, what seemed idiotic was that there are people to make war.

And there are such people, we aren't imagining it. Yesterday coming back from the funeral, I happened to say, "What fine sunshine! How warm it is!" Desrobert answered me, "It's not the sun that we're waiting for." Well, what is it then, imbecile? Maybe you'd like to tell me that it's freedom? Which one?

*N.R.F.* March 1, 1929, p.343: "If they want to make war again, there are many of us in France who will not march, who will not agree to march." Signed, Jean-Richard Bloch.

We should mobilize immediately (the Americans will take charge of this, I hope) and send off to war all those who are waiting for something other than the sun. Until they've gone through that ordeal they will ruin any peace.

*Saturday, April 29*

Tonight Mme. Ernst was arrested at the hotel. Yesterday the bus from Sisteron to Digne was robbed. At one o'clock, that is, in broad daylight, the bus was stopped on the road near Château-Arnoux. A man and a woman were killed in Sigonce in the middle of the village. Also it seems a Jew was gunned down here yesterday afternoon.

Luminous gray weather. Spring; toward the Rhône the sky is overcast. The rain never comes. We won't have fodder for the livestock and the wheat is turning brown before it ripens.

Started a little poem this morning almost without thinking about it.

*Monday, May 8*

Have since gone to Marseille. Beautiful days. But rough trip. The track destroyed at Bastides Blanches, two kilometers for the Manosque station. Bombs along the way at the canal bridge. Marseille clear and green but smelling very bad despite the high wind. It's an ocean spring there.

The attack in Voiron, sign of the times. A whole family shot dead from the eighty-year-old grandmother to a child, three years old, killed in its crib by *three* bullets in the neck and one in the belly. The murderers (what other word to use?) are students and teachers at the vocational school in the town! A group of Communist youths. Those children prepared for the murder by first becoming close friends with the family. That's how they learned the password that friends used to have the door opened. They came to spend a few friendly evenings with the family. One evening they came back, chatted nicely at first, then massacred everyone including the little one. They've been arrested. They've confessed. They say they had orders to kill. They'll be shot. These are the times we live in. All the teachers at the school are accomplices. The whole school is complicit and keeps quiet.

Hélène Laguerre wrote to me asking the reasons for my silence. I haven't sent the letter that I've copied out below:

"You imagine that something separates us other than my disgust at the position you've put me in where I must watch you working servilely in the disaster. It is strictly that. I gradually learned to detest all of you, such as you are, my old friends, and then came a kind of contempt that has me inhabiting a country you will never enter. That's all, and there's nothing else. I'm not happy to have lost you, but thus freed, I hardly consider you good enough to follow the Braumans whom you deserve. I left you as one leaves a valley inhabited by monsters. Those are the only reasons for my solitude and my silence. On the other hand, I like it very much when you write to me. Each time I wonder if I'll finally find a bit of that grandeur that I generously attributed to you all. Sadly, if you're the ones we must depend upon to reconstruct the world, what an infernal cesspool lies ahead of us. Thinking of you, I exhaust myself with prayers and appeals for a flood to submerge your endeavors for good. If the gods heard me, you'd stop dying on your feet, believe me."

*Thursday, May 11*

There has to be a revolution in Russia.

*Friday, May 12*

Two o'clock. I was going to lie down on the divan. Aline came running up the stairs: a German officer and a soldier down below. I heard Mémé calling Charles. I told Aline to have them come up. An officer and a soldier with a submachine gun enter. The officer salutes, approaches; he's come to have me sign two books, for him and his commander who he says is an archbishop! He emphasizes *archbishop*, then tells me that actually his commander is a protestant archbishop. A little later, the books signed, they leave. Frightening but no harm done.

Monday in Nyons the resistance surrounded the town and killed five people, among them Colombet of the Hôtel Colombet who made such good spelt in sauce and Dr. Gorgesco whom I knew at Lus-la-Croix-Haute.

Between a rock and a hard place. Odd situation. Who would believe that those two armed Germans who came to see me were drawn simply by literary legend? It would be hard to make the people of Manosque or anywhere else understand that. And to make them understand as well that I simply and coolly signed their books, nothing more. As I write this, Charles returns from his forced walk. I reassure him. Holding lives in outstretched arms, and on all sides, those who threaten to tickle you under the arm – with machine guns! Will I succeed in getting all my people across the waters?!

*Sunday, May 14*

Not a bad summary of my actions: "Swallowing the least possible number of toads." Which makes me stranger in my century than if I were dead. Because how they consume them! You'd think they liked them! This habitual diet that makes their nerves limp and their arteries watery.

I heard by telephone that the Marseille newspaper announced the dress rehearsal for *La Femme du boulanger* last evening at the Théâtre des Ambassadeurs. What good does that do? What I really need is a commercial success. Worries of this kind are returning after a break that followed the sale of my two manuscripts last January. I've been living on those sales until now. Nothing from Grasset and nothing from the *N.R.F* except 30,000 francs from the illustrated edition of *Chant du monde*. Already paid more than 60,000 francs in taxes this year. If the English attack and relations with Paris break down, I'm quickly going to find myself without money.

Very happy with *Deux cavaliers*. *Fragments* is getting better.

Gray-eyed weather. May dusty with celestial dust. Sky like a chalk road, hot. No rain. Concern over the wheat, and especially the fodder. If I want to keep my horses, I may have to sell my cows.

Tried to read F. Cooper. Impossible. Flat, contrived, entirely without interest. I can't understand why Balzac, Barbey d'Aurevilly, Stendhal, and Lamartine were infatuated with him. Reading Balzac, you get the sense that he would have liked to be Cooper. Fortunately that didn't happen. On the other hand, read the *Instructions nautiques* that finally arrived and – Hurray! There's the sea, the true sea, the vast sea, the winds, and the round earth. A large character: the sea; small characters: the sailors. The wracks, reefs, whales, moorings, and silence for the enormity of the waters.

I just saw a matinée of a film that made a deep impression on me and left me with that perfect contentment so rarely obtained from a cinematic work. I don't have the impression that it has ever met with great success, but I may be ill-informed on this point. It's *La Comédie du bonheur* by Marcel L'Herbier. Very beautiful and precise dialogue by Cocteau. At every instant, moving strokes of genius. It's a film that I would be very proud to have made. But how awful the theatre smelled! There was one matinée before the one that I went to at four o'clock. It stank like a lion cage. The odor you smell now in train cars and gathering places. Well, people decide to smell like what they are.

Just now summing up the work I've completed since the beginning of the war, I'm finding that, in terms of *numbers*, it's not negligible: I've written *Pour saluer Melville*, which is good, *Triomphe de la vie*, which is not as good. Two plays, *La Femme du boulanger* and *Le Voyage en calèche*. The latter will be good when I've redone the last scene in Act III. I've written the preface to *La Terre du voleur* and *Virgile*. And I've also written all the production notes, text, and action for *Le Chant du monde*, which I consider a major, perhaps even a great work, and that I would be happy to publish if Garganoff wasn't afraid of having it published. This year, I think I can successfully finish *Deux cavaliers*, write a few passages of *Fragments*, and begin writing *Grands chemins*. All things considered, maybe I could have worked better, but not more. And I've learned a lot.

Aline passed her baccalaureate and is going to study Philosophy. I'm delighted to see her embarking on something other than university culture. Because here, from now on, will be subjects for personal discussions. Oh, also, she knows how to present herself perfectly, clearly and carefully, before "*les études.*" She gave her account very intelligently.

*Thursday, May 18*

Yesterday evening returning from Forcalquier, Charles pointed out that once again *Signal* published a photo of me with no authorization on my part. Behavior motivated by a desire to force me to adopt a certain position or at least the appearance of that position. Which I absolutely refuse to do or let be done. I haven't good means to fight it. After thinking about it overnight, I've come up with the following solution: write a letter of protest to the editors of *Signal* (copy attached to these notes) and bring the case to the attention of a few friends through individual letters (copy of that letter and list of friends attached to these notes). Imagined last night the house invaded by submachine guns. In which case, I'd have to "go first," jump out of bed and go downstairs to meet them. That's the only way to protect Élise, my mother, and the children. But it's no fun to think about. Truly, I'm not very brave.

Nonetheless, I'd like to start writing the beginning of *Grands chemins* at least, as I had a wild desire to do so yesterday morning walking to Forcalquier by the big oak. Everything was clear and it was only a matter of writing it and I made a plan to sit down to write this evening instead of continuing to dictate *Fragments*, which I mean to let rest a little.

I've kept the *Signal* business from Élise. I'm sure that she would be frightened. This afternoon Mme. Meyssonnier told her about it. Élise's terror. I tried my best to reassure her. I can't reassure myself. The truth is I can no more be blamed for the appearance of that photo than for typhoid fever if I were to catch it. Wholly independent of my will. The risk of danger is indisputable. But I could bear it more easily if I were alone. Made a few arrangements this afternoon. The simplest way to reassure Élise would be to take her on a trip for eight or ten days, it doesn't matter where. But that's impossible with my old mother and my mother-in-law who would die of fear, and I understand that. At any given moment, Aline, who is with us, rebels and demands to stay near me. She nearly accuses her mother of making her leave for her own safety. She wants to stay here even though she's afraid. She says so. Evening comes and no one has made the least decision. Because what is there to decide? Perhaps to protect the children, send them to sleep at Mme. Meysonnier's house. A strange time. I imagine the Spanish Revolution must have started this way. That's what the Spaniard in Forcalquier said yesterday at noon. Another possible solution, my departure. Yes, but only on the condition that it would be enough to protect Élise and the children, because that's the whole question. That's the only question.

I don't know if I wrote down that last Friday in Paris, the thousandth performance of *Bout de la route* and the first performance of *La Femme du boulanger* took place at the same time.

At the end of *Deux cavaliers* Clef-des-Coeurs reappears. His fight in the chapter devoted to him is like Marceau's fight with the devil. That's why I will have him reappear to Marceau the victor near the village and at the end of the book to shape the conclusion. He introduces himself to Ariane as a friend of Marceau.

*Friday, May 19*

Discovered a book with an extraordinary style: Spanish tales by Scarron. Art with magical color. I found it this morning hidden in my library where I didn't know I had it. It carried me back to his *Roman comique* that cast a spell over my youth, as well as *Histoire de Francion*, and I realized that there, as in Fielding, is where I'll find the initial dynamism I need to begin writing *Les Grand chemins*. Today I'm taking great pleasure in reading these texts, imitations but so originally French: light and multicolored. How vastly superior to *L'Astrée*. Almost as great (in style) as Cervantes. Maybe greater (in style). I was equally moved once again this morning by some passages in La Bruyère. There's a whole region in my library that I'm going to revisit with pleasure.

During the night Élise was horribly frightened by the slightest creak. She made me get up at two in the morning to do the rounds. Which I did to make her happy, but cursing as I went because I had just fallen asleep.

*Friday, May 19*

Élise is very frightened but very brave. She's proposing that I go into hiding and she will stay here. But no, no.

Scarron calls the Jews *modern Christians.*

*Saturday, May 20*

Last night Élise was terror-stricken. She was crying hard. I held her in my arms and reassured her. After a little while, she fell asleep.

This afternoon the announced visit from the bishop, accompanied by a nurse – who addressed him as "*tu*" no less. A man with bright eyes under enormous dark eyebrows. He speaks of gentleness and peace, but makes war; of disaster, apocalypse, and at one point his eyes even fill with tears. It was embarrassing.

Finally, rain. The sky black and angry, wind, heavy slanting showers, and that beautiful dark rain in the green leaves, so dear to my heart. Glorious scents and from all sides the sound of pouring rain that drenches the trees and fields. We need a very long, very hard storm.

Since returning from Forcalquier I've done no work. Stopped a bit by worries and especially by the difficulty of what I must write: the fight between Marceau and Clef-des-Coeurs. What I've done doesn't measure up to what precedes it, and the means by which to heighten it all have yet to appear.

*Friday, May 26*

Yesterday at noon an alert that lasted two hours. Apparently they bombarded Carnoules. This morning at ten another alert. The light is beautiful. Golden spring. No sound of planes. Clear, powder blue sky; a light veil of mist in the distance and all outward signs of an opulent peace.

Work is picking up again in *Deux cavaliers*. The second battle between the man and Marceau gave me a lot of trouble. I think the benefit now is that it's making me see soberly but clearly. I have stubbornly sought that clarity through these days that are difficult from every perspective.

I'm reading a very beautiful book in English that hasn't been translated: *Turning Wheels* by Stuart Cloete. Fleshy, wild, and dense. I will let Gallimard know about it but don't have the time to translate it.

Stopped work on *Fragments*. Decided to begin writing *Grands chemins* and to translate *Joseph Andrews* by Fielding. Exhausting myself with work to achieve the peace of the mole.

More and more I'm immersed in a very great solitude. I can't say that it weighs on me. It goes well with such a taste for unsociability. But from time to time I have rushes of joy that are very hard to contain.

*Saturday, May 27*

Last night at midnight, an alert and a large fleet of planes could be heard flying over. This morning at nine, another alert. It's eleven o'clock now and for the last two hours we can hear and see an enormous fleet of more than a thousand white and black planes flying from the east to the northwest. For the last two hours the noise hasn't let up and every minute someone notices and points out new groups that rise, wings wide, from the chestnut leaves.

Some squadron units pass directly over us. There's a moment of silence, then new rumbles rising from the south now, coming closer and closer.

A strange dream last night. We were in Switzerland at a hotel. Élise was there. I was condemned to death along with another man, a stranger, and I could see only his hands and torso. He was sitting at the corner of a table. M. Chaumeton (from Manosque) brought us the hemlock in a bowl. He told me that they had added sugar for me. Actually it was a lumpy green jam that I ate calmly with a spoon. Tasted good, moreover. Everything happened very peacefully with hardly any death throes. I made a few arrangements with Élise on the subject of the money from my manuscripts, without tears or gnashing of teeth. The hotel owner came to inform me obligingly that there was a discreet exit for funeral processions. At that moment a procession for a Swiss notable passed by under my window, accompanied by a choir of young girls and a line of cows. I insisted upon a similar ceremony. It was promised to me. At that point we began to walk with Élise. Remembering Socrates I told her that it would begin with my legs growing cold. I apologized to Élise for my thoughtlessness, explaining to her that throughout my life my work had required that I cultivate passions and lyric outbursts.

I wrapped my cape around Élise and we walked side by side. We wanted to climb a steep embankment. My legs began to grow weak. But I kept going with the help of a camping knife I stuck in the ground. Mme. Talenti had given it to me, but in the dream it seemed to be a gift from Élise since I told her that the knife was one of the most beautiful things in my life. After that, I was in Manosque and I went into a tobacco shop – that old tobacco shop owned by Mme. Chaix and old Héloïse where I would go as a child to buy my father his two ounces of tobacco. There the dream faded. I was still condemned to death but I began to doubt the effects of the hemlock.

This evening we learned that Marseille was bombed this morning. Only hearsay because the phone lines between here and Marseille are cut, and there's no newspaper either. Guy whom I sent to the station for information on the fate of his mother returned with the news that the station is cut off from everything as well. Everything seems to indicate that this time it's true. They're claiming that bombs fell in the center of the city; they're saying Boulevard National, but that isn't the center. Will try the radio tonight.

Haven't written anything. Succeeded in really envisioning and composing the "Clef-des-Coeurs" chapter, but not able to write a line. To top it all off, it's essential that I start the translation of *Joseph Andrews* as quickly as possible. I would have done that yesterday if I hadn't been half blinded by one of those irritations in my right eye that I suffer and that each time makes me feel like I'm living at the bottom of the sea. I see everything through salt water. Followed by a headache and nervous twitches in my eyelids. Very unpleasant. Continued reading with pleasure *Roman comique*.

Élise calls me. The radio is reporting 600 dead and 1,000 wounded in Marseille. The bombs fell on the center of the city. La Canebière, they say, in particular.

*Sunday, May 28*

Eight o'clock in the morning. I arrived at the post office where I went to telegraph L. and P. Many women sending telegraphs as well. The disaster in Marseille seems catastrophic. It was the whole inoffensive center of the city that was heavily bombed. La Canebière is on fire. The Maupetit bookstore must be burning. Worried about L., with his office at 44, and the Barthélemies, with their store close by. Rue de Rome. Rue de Rome is burning too. Bombs hit the central post office, a few dozen meters from the Hôtel de Paris where I usually stay. They're talking about many thousands dead. I think it's the first center of a large city to be bombed in France. Rue Beauveau is burning. All the small streets perpendicular to La Canebière are affected. I'm thinking of all my friends, the Aviérinos, Fluchère, the Barthélemies, whose lives may be completely shaken to their very roots, so far from the war. And how are they going to be able to leave? And it's impossible for me to go help them: no trains until Tuesday.

Also yesterday morning when the planes passed over they dropped bombs on Forcalquier. Why? To jettison them? Why right over Forcalquier when there are a hundred square kilometers of open land right next to it? Why not imagine the sadism of the bomber who sees below him the beautiful, peaceful green countryside that I'm looking at this morning from my window. His modern response is to open the bomb doors. If one isn't careful, it's easy to fall prey to the various propagandas: those claims that the airmen are "drunk niggers" or, if they're English, they're scared shitless. No one has normal responses. This morning, the Sunday of Pentecost, is the first communion here. Tidying up, women in their Sunday best; when I went down to the post office, they were hosing off the terraces of the cafés.

Beautiful light. In the meadow far below, men in white shirts slowly raking the hay.

The world seems to be collapsing into a general lack of quality.

In 1939–40 I was writing in *Chute de Constantinople*... "and their cries when they lose their footing in the abyss!"

*Monday, May 29*

(I often get the date wrong; yesterday was the 28th.) A telephone call late yesterday reassured me about E. and A. Safe and sound in Marseille. E. had gone down to *take shelter* in the hallway of the apartment building, but between two strikes he ran to hide in tunnel of the Gare de l'Est. He seemed very upset on the phone. He called me again this morning, still very shaken. A. as well. He repeated, "It's a massacre, a massacre." G. P. telephoned, too, to reassure me he was alright, he and Nini are both alive, and he also repeated, "It's a massacre." He reported more than 2,000 dead and more than 5,000 wounded. Because of his position, those figures are more accurate than the ones announced officially.

It rained, rather late in the day. A small storm. The sound of it seemed extremely peaceful. It brought comfort and peace. It was reassuring. It was ahistorical.

Incapable of working. It's irritating. Tomorrow, somehow or other, without fail, I have to force myself to get to work on *Joseph Andrews* and *Deux cavaliers*; *Fragments* can be put off until later, if I return to it at all. It may be a mistake that I'm getting over.

Ten dead in Forcalquier! Why? It's so obviously stupid that the toadies claim it was a German fighter who did the bombing. I'd rather think it was sadism. No, I don't distinguish between Germans and Anglo-Americans, one is the same as the other. The Germans machine-gunned those who were fleeing; the Anglo-Americans bombed Forcalquier for the fun of it. Hatred for green pastures, no doubt. They've simply found a substitute for love finally, something that takes its place, does not deceive (for the time being).

*Thursday, June 1*

I went to Margotte yesterday afternoon. Bombs fell 200 meters from the farm the other day. Mme. Salomé, the children, uncle, and aunt were thrown flat on their bellies in the fields. In

Forcalquier, which is five kilometers from there, eleven bombs fell. Eyewitnesses say that they were all dropped by a plane that had broken off from the squadron and just circled above the town. In the police station, which was destroyed, an officer's wife, looking out the window at the planes streaming over and talking to another woman on the street, exclaimed, "It's the landing; this isn't unlucky; I tell you there's going to be one hell of a celebration." Five minutes later she was crushed, she and her three children dead. The same squadron dropped bombs randomly over its entire route: Riez, Rians, Vinon, Valensole, Saint-Maime, Forcalquier, Vachères, Simiane, Banon, Saint-Christofol, Sault, everywhere. I received a letter from Thoret this morning and he also talks about sadism. In any case, as an expert on aviation, and what an expert, he's hard on the flight crews. A few more strikes like this and sympathy for the Anglo-Americans is going to shift. But maybe they will be the ones to save Europe despite themselves. It would be quite fitting (considering the general spinelessness and filth) if it were filth and spinelessness that finally produced the great liberation movements. Because if we waited for grandeur…!

What *Fragments* lacks is *form*, that's all – period.

*Saturday, June 3*

I now have the same money worries as in January. The sale of the two manuscripts was only enough for us to live on for six months. I can't make a living. I'm going to have to sell other manuscripts. If I can do that. Otherwise, sell a farm.

My mother is sick and can't breathe.

I have to redo *Fragments* in a form that allows for grand poetic departures. But I need time.

Yesterday in broad daylight, men armed with submachine guns broke into the law office of M. Borel, made him sign a check for the full amount in his bank account, accompanied him to the bank, took 300,000 francs and ran off. In the center of town, at ten o'clock in the morning. Ach. the teacher, the gang leader apparently, was walking around with a gun in plain sight, hanging from a belt under his jacket, and the day before yesterday, men from a rival gang fired at his automobile three kilometers from Manosque. He escaped. It seems there are several gangs: Ach.'s gang, Mar.'s gang. Mar.'s gang just raided a garage for its gasoline six days ago. They took the gasoline and paid saying, "We aren't

Ach.'s gang, we're another one." But no one knows if it was the same gang that robbed the oil reserves; without paying that time.

With the heat, it seems there's an unbearable stench of corpses in Marseille. More than two thousand are still in the process of rotting under the rubble.

*Sunday, June 4*

Ten o'clock in the morning, the alert sounds. Immediately followed by violent rumbling at the far end of town, then silence. We're listening. The most beautiful possible weather. Sun, powder blue sky, a little cool, light wind. Since the other day when ten bombs fell a hundred meters from Margotte, the hens have laid only small eggs, hardly bigger than quail eggs; they have no yolks. Imagine the panic there must be in Marseille now. All is quiet for the moment.

*Tuesday, June 6*

Charles returns from town with news. First, the Germans are said to have arrived. He didn't see a single one, but someone told him that they had commandeered a villa on Boulevard Saint-Lazare. Then, the landing has supposedly begun. Where, when, how, no one knows. There's no trace of it, no indication, but it has begun, no doubt about it. A collective hallucination? Anyone declaring in the empty city today that the Germans haven't arrived and the landing hasn't taken place would be torn to pieces.

Cool weather, clouds, overcast sky, crosswinds, still no rain.

Yesterday Mme. X. arrived. For at least three months she's left me in perfect peace. "If I don't come anymore," she said, "it's because I'm afraid of becoming attached to you." She makes stupid faces. I answer dryly, "There's no danger of that." She protests. I move on and consider how to drive her away.

Began working on *Deux cavaliers* again.

Serious money worries. Still nothing from Paris, no letters. Wrote to Dambournet, L'Argus du Livre, to propose selling three manuscripts to him, *Batailles dans la montagne*, *Le Poids du ciel*, *Les Vraies richesses*.

A difficult period to get through morally. What I would need is to succeed at some incontestably beautiful work. What I'm writing doesn't satisfy me. Not enough real work even though I stay shut up in my office the whole day. Irritated by difficulties that I can't seem to overcome. I've hardly written more than a few pages for weeks. And even those aren't as good as the ones I was writing three months ago.

Decided to give up tobacco, I smoked my last bag of it. I won't buy anymore on the black market. Totally eliminating personal expenses.

Noon. So, it's true. The landing at least. Fighting southwest of Le Havre, we learn from a badly broken up radio broadcast.

Camoin came to see me this evening at about seven o'clock. I told him about all the mistakes that Vigroux made in his translation of *Joseph Andrews*. Camoin told me they killed Ach. Pétain and Laval speaking on the radio about the landing. The bad days have come. According to Camoin, 11,000 (eleven thousand) planes supposedly participated in the attack. Insane times! What's going to become of us? That's what they keep asking below, my mother, my wife, my mother-in-law, shelling peas for canning.

It's what I'm asking myself as I write this note.

The wind has turned to the north and is blowing in gusts. Sick today. Even the light is agonizing.

A crystal clear day. The mistral has swept away all the fog. From here the hills on the far side of the valley look close enough to touch. I can make out juniper bushes on the Mirabeau hills and, more than fifty kilometers away, the details of the rock face at Sainte-Victoire. I didn't listen to the radio at seven o'clock. It was on very loud below but I wasn't up, and only got up later when the telephone rang. It was Mme. Meyssonnier leaving for Mison for the funeral of a cousin who was crushed by the train, to tell us she would probably return this evening by train, if there was one. We are looking after her daughter in the meantime and will be for quite some time, I imagine. We also have André with us whose wife left for her son's first communion in Banassac, hasn't been heard from since, and must have broken down somewhere. There are no more trains, no more letters, no more telephone. In addition to the family, I'm now responsible for little Marguerite, André, and Guy. We're considering the possibility of having to take refuge at the Criquet farm. Aline, Guy, and I would leave on bicycle, the women in the cart, and André and Charles on foot. For the moment, I calm them down and make them stay here. There's absolutely no reason to rush off madly on adventures, as if to a picnic. The idea that we'll have to learn to be nomads again fills the children with joy, and the adults as well. As long as the danger is far away. It is still far away. Apparently the fighting is furious and the outcome is far from decided. Those at the head of the Anglo-American front near Saint-Vaast were thrown into the sea. The other front, on the contrary, seems to be growing.

Getting to work. And being careful about knowing too much or going too deeply into the science of things. Martel's example. Retaining a freshness of heart and hands. That's difficult.

Ten o'clock. The siren is sounding. Even so, the wind is terrible.

*Thursday, June 8*

Yesterday afternoon I went to Margotte by bicycle. The land empty, the world empty; it seemed like an empty Sunday. I passed households fleeing, one after another, belongings heaped precariously in trucks, heading for Marseille. At Bois d'Asson, the mine wasn't operating. I learned at Margotte that the terrorists had forced the workers to close it. At the crossroads, groups of young men idly swinging their arms. The sweet smell of linden trees in full blossom tossed by the wind. When I arrived at Margotte,

Mme. Salomé told me immediately that the Anglo-Americans had taken Paris. It turns out she had mixed up what she heard on the radio, that they were in Boulogne, but: -sur-Mer. As for Salomé, he went to look at his automobile, out of gas now for four years. He told me that he was going to go have it serviced immediately. He's expecting the return of 1936 before long. The return to before the war. It would be useless to try to make him understand first of all, that wouldn't be enough, and secondly, it probably won't happen, and finally, that what will happen will only happen after horrible catastrophes. He caresses his auto, jubilant, and all ready to dive back into any post-war whatsoever, so long as he has gasoline and can rev up his engine and go back-firing down the roads.

Returned home about seven o'clock. On the dissident radio station, they're giving orders for civil war to the gendarmes, the jailers, and even the resistance fighters. They're ordering them to take to the maquis with weapons and supplies and to open the prison doors.

As I'm writing this down this morning, Ch. arrives from town with news. The reports are strange and contradictory. Groups of maquis fighters have supposedly seized the town hall, the post office, and the police station. But he saw armed Germans at the town hall, the post office is functioning, and the police chief, whom I know to be a Francist, is still there. More news from Charles: fighting in Sainte-Tulle. Now from my window I can see Sainte-Tulle which, at six kilometers away, is in clear sight. It's calm, peaceful, not a sound coming from it. Third piece of news: the Anglo-Americans are supposed to have landed at Cette. Élise is nervous and asks me if we shouldn't leave for Criquet. I don't think so. Why do that? Let's wait. It's through obeying last evening's orders that the game will be played. To what extent and in what fashion will the country obey? And on the other hand, what is there to fear?

In any case and as a precaution, I told Guy, who was heading to Criquet by bike to get milk, not to leave. And I advised Ch. simply to return to town to get enough bread for a small supply for us.

I'm doing my best to continue working on *Deux cavaliers*.

After leaving again for town, Charles returns. Now he's saying that the dissidents didn't take the town hall last night, but they came to arm those who were members of the organizations (that seems true, or at least plausible). On the other hand, the prefecture's office in Digne was supposedly stormed. But then I wonder why there aren't new administrators already. I just had a calm telephone call from Blavette who asked me to meet him this afternoon, so the post office is alright. Real news: a German was killed tonight at the public house and a police officer killed himself while loading his gun badly. Waiting.

I destroyed three bad pages of *Deux cavaliers* written over the past few days.

Mme. Meyssonier returned from Mison last evening. She had to go fifteen or twenty kilometers on foot, just this side of Sisteron, before meeting a truck that left her not far from here, where she was able to find help again.

*Friday, June 9*

After a day of true madness yesterday, today promises to be calmer. It seems someone was pulling the wool over our eyes. Last night everyone in town left their houses and went to camp in the hills. The rumors circulating predicted terrible, mysterious events for the night. André and Angèle came to spend the night with us. There were huge numbers of false reports, each more outrageous than the last. By the end of last evening there was not a single cool head among us. I had to reprimand Guy, calmly and sensibly, for wanting to take extreme measures. Today everything is back to square one. In my opinion, a premature attempt, one of those terrible blunders that's enough to destroy the best of causes. A lack of cool heads in the command. It seems the real leaders were very displeased that these initiatives were taken. It seems to be confirmed as well that all this unrest was only regional. So I was seeing things clearly when I advised caution. Why can't we be more English in the good sense: "Wait and see."

Guy is determined despite what I said to him, and I told him that if he had been too quick to accept my reasons, I wouldn't respect him as I do. One must lose one's illusions as quickly as possible, so, yes, go where you can lose them the fastest. That's the law of war. For the moment, all they see is a big country outing. In place of the old "unfolding of things," now there's the appeal of cowboy and gangster movies. Big House, Zorro, sports. Obeying the rush of blood. Permission to play a grand version of cops and robbers. A big playground. What an idiot I was to write *Le Grand troupeau*. The simplest solution is to calmly accept that butcher shops exist, and even to go there to buy good meat.

Yesterday, thirteen dead in Forcalquier, according to rumors. Those who went to occupy the town hall, or I don't know what, clashed with, I don't know, either the Germans or the militia who killed thirteen of them.

"What I want most of all," says Guy, "is equipment." The desire for a parachute harness. Not once, it must be acknowledged, do they speak sentimentally, as in 93, 48, or 70. They are thrilled with (laugh at) the idea of jumping. Not one speaks of grandeur or country. Oh, no. Never of country. These are political armies built on the misconceptions of youth who want to practice piano in china shops.

It's a beautiful day, clear, full of color, a little wind.

I understand all that very well. I just don't like it, that's all. Behind them are others who want to be brought armchairs so they can die sitting down, from old age, cancer, their prostate.

Still no real news about the landing. Neither the English nor the Germans.

*Saturday, June 10*

Finally it's cloudy and overcast. It hasn't rained yet but the humid air already offers relief to the body, relaxes it. Peace, and the songs of birds. Nightingales are calling in the tall chestnut trees.

My neighbor Maurel, a miner at the coal mine in Gaude, hasn't returned. He's been dragooned, surely against his own wishes. He's peace-loving, a gardener, family man, conformist, easily astounded by the tiny flash of a lighter. What purpose does it serve to make a man like this into a soldier? If this picnic lasts a few days he'll hold out, but all the time thinking of his daughter, wife, rabbits, hens, his garden, and his new potatoes. But this is certainly not the man to fire the last shots. If the country holiday lasts too long, he'll end up saying to himself, "Now let's move on to serious things." And he'll return to the bosom of his family.

The young men, like Guy, don't talk about battles, combat, fighting, they talk about "scuffles." "There are terrific scuffles." They don't want to fight but to "scuffle." In one sense, that's to see clearly, already.

It's raining hard, a beautiful heavy rain. My limbs feel light and well-oiled. My head feels at ease in the humidity. Despite new troubles, my eyes take great physical pleasure in looking at the dark blue day. The sound of rain is pleasing to my ears like music and suddenly, having taken up a book, I see magical seeds bursting forth from all sides.

In addition to the thirteen young men killed on the square in front of the church in Forcalquier, there was a drama at the police station. Captain Faucon killed the son of the police captain who wanted to arrest him and the police captain killed Captain Faucon. As for the young men, they were from the Bois d'Asson mine and still following that insane plan, they were occupying the town hall, pure and simple. A truckload of Germans arrived. The young miners advanced, naively thinking that, at the sight of their friendly faces, it would all be settled, pure and simple (which was stupid!). They were massacred. Two minutes later, absolute calm "reigned at Varsovie." What madness! Who organized all this stupidity? Who pulled the wool over our eyes *in the first place*? Salomé, who told me all this, has backed off from his revolutionary declarations. He's already recanting them.

It's been clearly confirmed that this unrest was strictly regional and hasn't spread beyond the district.

Four o'clock in the afternoon. The sun's out again.

*Sunday, June 11*

Fresh wind from the north, clear sky, bright sun, good cheer, clear horizons, you can see the pines on the hill twenty kilometers away. Great indifference generally for the aborted attempts of the last few days. Once more, the dead are dead. I had hung hams in the storeroom where I was keeping my supply of flour and spelt and they've been infested by weevils. A. Michel is in the process of fumigating them using laurel from the garden. Twice I've lent 4,000 francs to A. Michel who doesn't work and must send shoes to his son Jacques in Germany. Despite my huge money worries at the moment. No chance of seeing them end, just the opposite.

I'm beginning to see a very small way out of my struggles with that difficult passage in *Deux cavaliers* that I've worked and reworked more than five or six times this week. This morning I'm catching a glimpse of it.

Began to read some Balzac: *La Muse du département*. As every time, moved. Perhaps I'll be able to work today.

Had a visit the other day from Germaine Bellec who has set up a tailor shop in Céreste. I told her that I was thinking of all those phonies in the Contadour. Of whom she is one. Because how she squirmed, turning all her kindness sour as she explained that she still loved me, but.... Why *still* and why *but*? I told her why: because I was too generous with her and with them all. No burden is more unpleasant than gratitude. Nothing is more invigorating that ingratitude. At least have the frankness to acknowledge it. For my part, I acknowledge that I was stupid and very childish with them. But now that I know, I have no pity. Don't count on my weakness anymore. You cannot imagine how cruel I am now; keep your distance and stay on your guard; at least I'm giving you warning. And I say this to your face.

Renée, Maurel's little girl, came to play with Sylvie at noon. She repeats what she hears and when asked if she has news about her father she tells us, "They are marching on Valensole!" !! I've never witnessed a more peaceful day.

Chinese proverb: *If all the idiots wore white hats, the street would resemble a bed of lilies.*

Two hours later I heard Renée coming into the garden saying, "My papa has returned."

Mémé returned from the hospital where she went to see Aunt Noémie (still recovering from her colostomy but still alive despite that infamous cancer *this* big). They wouldn't let Mémé enter. They were in the midst of carrying in the wounded. Men in groups were talking about an engagement along the Durance where there were ten deaths. Engagement with whom? Against whom? And most importantly, why? Especially since, despite everything, these deaths and those in Forcalquier, there's an atmosphere of general indifference, as I've said. Apart from indifference, there's fear. Right now a babe in arms would understand that all of this is premature.

*Monday, June 12*

No real news about the slaughter last evening except from Dr. Petit who tells me the casualty is going to die. Last evening they said that Marg. had been killed. As in Forcalquier, it was the Germans who opened fire on the men and boys who were "guarding" the bridge. They've confirmed only that six are dead. There is so much confusion that this morning M. Camoin, an otherwise intelligent man, told Aline that Barcelonnette was occupied by the Italian resistance led by English officers who parachuted down. We're used to seeing salvation descend from the skies. The

Italians! Tell me that we're supposed to rejoice over help from the Italians, when hardly a year ago we couldn't find sarcasm enough to commemorate their national cowardice. Now they tell us, "But there are Italian resisters!" Once again we need that Chinese proverb.

Better work on *Deux cavaliers*, I'm finally out of the "Clef-des-Coeurs" chapter and beginning the next one: "Conte d'hiver."

*Thursday, June 15*

Yesterday at Margotte I heard about the atrocities committed by the armed miners from the Bois d'Asson mine. They killed a woman who was said to be spying. She was receiving 50,000 francs each month through the mail, Salomé told me. Which is the exact and only evidence for this invented charge. They pursued her for a whole day, a hundred armed men against one defenseless woman, making her cross and recross the Largue where she was in water up to her waist. Finally they shot and killed her with their submachine guns, then they undressed her and "carried her into a little cabin," Salomé said discreetly. Then they dragged her naked body onto the road and finally they ripped it apart with grenades.

Last Sunday, those same miners combed the countryside around Saint-Maime-Dauphin to find recruits among the farmers. Not one joined them. They were all turned away with this beautiful peasant expression: *We have work to do.* This is exactly what demonstrates that there truly is a peasant civilization (despite Guéhenno's claim in Pourrat's *Vent de mars*). And this is also where the sickle and the hammer part ways. Salomé has changed his tune. Armed gangs are looting the farmers. He's even talking, already, of resisting with the farmhands, trying to seize machine guns to fire at the others. He's also talking about all the farms joining together. At the exact moment that I had predicted (*Chute de Constantinople* written in 1939, published in *L'Eau vive* – and published expressly to mark the date) the anticipated peasant reaction is taking place exactly like a chemical reaction. Proof of a substance so pure that its behavior can be mathematically predicted.

Alert at 11:30. Immediately, passing right over the trees and houses, ten to twelve planes flying from Pierrevert, southwest. No telling what nationality. Surprising that they are so low.

Received four letters from Paris this evening.

I just read *Le Cabinet des antiques* by Balzac. I wasn't familiar with this book. It's very beautiful. It is so intensely captivating at the end that one willingly follows the whole digression on the first supreme magistracy. And even, in passing, is happy to learn that the stairway leading from Blondet's garden to his pelargonium hothouse has thirteen steps. And had the complete history of the weaving of his cotton hood been included, one would happily go through any first magistracy again, with eagerness and ardor. So magical is the driving impulse. But, be careful: don't imitate. It's Balzac. Acknowledge, admire, but don't try to do it: we are only ordinary humans.

The letter from a friend relates Marcel Pagnol's plot against *La Femme du boulanger*. I really couldn't give a damn. If he thinks that I don't know my play isn't as good as his film dialogue, he's wrong. I'm perfectly aware of that.

*Friday, June 16*

Many dead bodies are being found in the woods on the other side of the Durance where the skirmish took place last Sunday. Everywhere the dissidents seem to have randomly dropped their weapons and fled. They're claiming about a hundred such deaths. But that seems exaggerated. This morning forty truckloads of

German troops, that is, almost a thousand men, passed through heading toward Valensole, asking the way.

Warm and humid, a storm brewing. I am hardly working at all. Nevertheless I know very well that it must be done and I can produce the ordinary whenever. It's the extraordinary that doesn't come. Patience, I myself seem to need the rain. I'm beginning to receive letters from Paris again. Received a letter this morning from the Red Cross pertaining to the suitcase with personal effects that I had sent to Mme. Ernst, and that couldn't be delivered. My second mailing, on the other hand, seems to have arrived at her address.

The newspaper is reporting executions of resisters, 180 in Lambesc, 110 in Valréas near Nyons, 30 in Vaison, and here, who knows how many when the truckloads of troops that came through this morning reach the countryside?

Already excessively hot. And the irritating drone of cicadas. And this burning yellow country that I hate. The need for water, for rain, humidity, blue, deep greens, the scent of mushrooms.

I'm continually reassessing my old friendships. Lucien Jacques's visit was only a flash of lightning, and the tone of his note to thank me for sending him *La Terre du voleur* is certainly not what I'd expect after the last twenty years. Have reached a point (or he made me reach it) where I will surely strike him from my heart as well, and be relieved to do so.


*Thursday, June 22*

A few letters from friends in Paris with information on the conspiracy of critiques mounted by Pagnol regarding *La Femme du boulanger*. What I can see most clearly is that he has exceeded his goal, having pushed too far. Too much unanimity – which Jemet points out in his article in *Germinal* – clearly the party line since one of the critiques says *word for word* what Cocteau said to Alice Cocéa a few days before the premier and what J. Cuisine quoted to me. And this doesn't really affect me.

I must rework *Le Voyage.* Instead of telling, show it, so end the first act where it used to end, and begin the second act with the scene of the informer at Prina's. *Show* what John the servant tells in scene three of the second act. I'm going to do that work very quietly without telling anyone about it. My first act is good because I did it quietly without opinions or advice, unhurried. The rest is bad because I was pushed around, tormented by deadlines, requests, suggestions. But first, finish *Deux cavaliers.*

Gustave R.'s tales of the resistance and the botched "Sicilian Vespers" were going down well outside the café yesterday. He didn't mind at all speaking right out. He saw it, he said, the cowards in the bushes, the drunks. The resisters who gathered on the Gréoulx square and who finally cheered for the marshall after a short speech by a German officer. This pettiness and spinelessness I really want to believe is purely regional. Too bad that R. is a collaborator (so they say): he's Paul Reynaud's cousin. No: he is a true adventurer; he knows all about it; he doesn't acknowledge his own. Like me, he says that all those brave men thought they were going on some giant picnic with circus games. But when they felt that they'd become part of the circus, they let out such a cry that no one would give them back their seats in the bleachers, under the tents, or in the hammocks for afternoon naps.

Gallimard is always ready to do me a favor, with unfailing kindness. He answered my letter immediately and sent 20,000 francs that he may not even owe me. Grasset hasn't sent me the 70,000 that he almost owes me, I say "almost" because he is about to release the special edition of *Que ma joie demeure* and *Pan* that will sell for 2,500 francs a copy. I asked him to pay me the royalties a few days in advance. Gallimard paid me for *Le Chant du monde*, and not just a few days in advance but maybe a few years.

A dream the other night: someone says to me, "Look, this is your son. You've just had a son." I don't know if it was Élise. The boy is astonishingly handsome, already grown like Sylvie. So beautiful! To shout about! Gold like the sun, slender, with the face of a god.

"Let there be positioned at the four corners of Europe four energetic men, knowing what they want and having determined what means of action to employ, and let them raise their voices and arms at the same time, and the whole place will go up in dust like a cloud of smoke."

Metternich

(Vienna, January 6, 1832)

Yesterday I sent Guy to the Criquet farm to get supplies, especially milk and maybe a hen. As usual he went there with his friend Henri Bonnet. I advised Guy to get back early. But by ten-thirty he still wasn't here, which made me nervous, but I assumed he'd gotten held up at the Bonnets' and I went to bed. By eleven o'clock (and by then I was very worried because the curfew is at ten), the bell rang. I heard Guy come in, very excited, and I heard what he was saying, "Do I have some stories to tell." He began talking loudly in the dining room below. Immediately Aline and Sylvie ran up to my room. They said that Guy found a corpse on the road near Criquet and it was Roger-Paul Bernard! I can't believe it! I got up immediately. Roger-Paul Bernard! The gentle young poet, with a great talent all his own, that young printer in Pertuis who was so devoted to me, whom I loved so much, so touching in his young enthusiasm for art, that boy with the face of a girl who was married a year ago to a woman so thin that between the two of them they had only forty years and weighed hardly eighty kilos. At the time when he was called to leave for Germany, he put his trust in me and came from Pertuis by taxi with his father to ask for my advice. If he had followed the advice I gave him, I have the sad satisfaction of telling myself, he wouldn't be dead. He was shot point-blank with a revolver, the bullet entering below his eye near his nose. He was splayed across the road, dead, alone, near the Viens train station. He'd been killed about nine o'clock that morning. It was ten o'clock when Guy and Bonnet found him. They had just been stopped in Cereste by some Germans who searched them, saying that they'd killed one of their comrades (because Guy and Bonnet are the right age and look like resisters) because he had a pistol in his bag. The pistol was lying there on the café table. Finding everything in order, the Germans released Guy and Bonnet and it was when they set off again down the road that they found Bernard whose abandoned body was already covered with flies. Bonnet took the risk of unfolding the dead man's arm from across his chest and removing his wallet. He had on him coded messages similar to those broadcast on dissident radio, Guy said. At the moment I wondered if this wasn't simply one of Bernard's poems, it's so hard for me to imagine the young boy I knew taking this stand. But according to what Guy maintained, there's no doubt, they really were coded messages. That and the pistol! Poor young, sensitive, enthusiastic boy; so open, so ready to trust, to believe, to offer himself; so bright, so beautiful when he came to introduce his little wife to me. She has a two-month old baby now. He'd rented a little house near the Criquet farm. He was living there with his family, his wife and baby, with forty-five years between the three of them now and maybe ninety kilos altogether. Writing poems and a novel with his great, amazing, extremely individual talent. The most distinct among all the young writers I know. With a beautiful, astounding future, going out among the people and destined to become a great poet. I can just see him, the day he came to ask my advice. A little surprised that I advised caution, which his father approved. And him unyielding, and me saying to him, "Now that I've told you what I think you must do, I remain your friend whatever you decide and will help you as much as I can." Advising him to stay out of it all. Above all, no weapons, I insisted. And he said to me, "Oh yes, of course, no weapons. I simply want to write." And now, the pistol, the messages, a bullet through his head, his corpse abandoned on the road near the Viens station.

I wanted to retain a little doubt about the identity of the body. I kept telling myself that maybe it wasn't Bernard, the identification having come through hearsay and no one seeing the body except Guy and Bonnet who didn't know him. But this morning Bonnet came and showed me the photo he'd taken from the wallet and yes, I'm afraid it really is Bernard.

We are in a kind of ghastly China.

This morning a visit from Champsaur. We talked about this war that has already been won by Russia socially and by America industrially. All that remains is to see who will win militarily. We should have been able to claim the great spiritual victory. But we never realized that for great victories, M. Déroulède isn't a great enough philosopher.

Make France into a quality Switzerland. When a Frenchman puts three words with three words, it isn't long before he creates something of international value. Likewise if he puts red next to green or if he arranges the notes of the scale in his own style. Unrivaled products with which France could (and perhaps will) dominate the other victors. In any case, share in the victory. All other industries could be dominated by its slogans. It could seize hold of the minds of the people as they leave the factories, could dominate all their free time, could offer spiritual pleasures worldwide. What more could one desire. That is the highest place. That is the top position. Others work; France expresses and therefore dominates, creates, directs. Regiments and armies of invincible artists. But don't let the poets waste their time playing with pistols and secret messages.

*Sunday, June 25*

This morning at ten o'clock the alert sounded. At the same time you could hear the roar of big squadrons. The sky is heavily overcast; you look and can't see anything. It seemed like the squadrons were just passing over the Rhône valley, to the west of us. Flying south to north. The noise increased rapidly and then diminished and died. Fifteen minutes later the noise began again north to south, still to the west, but closer to us this time. A few planes passed right over our region. The noise died. Then it started up again from west to east over the Valensole plateau, fading in the east. Sunday alerts are so frequent now that there's an expression for them: the American is going to mass.

Luckily, I've relocated the article that Wullens wrote against me. I will not write a single word in response. If all my friends whose quotes he uses against me are fair-minded, it's up to them to respond. Alfred Campozet, H.V. the postal worker in Marseille, all those who were part of the Contadour in September 1939. Gogois, the comrade in Nice who was waiting for his wife. Those who left for Switzerland and in general, all those mixed up with me in September 1939. I haven't said a word. But they must speak. It's very simple. When they've spoken the honest truth about what happened, there won't be much left of Wullen's claims. But I won't say a word. I'm keeping the article with my documents and simply noting where the truth can actually be found.

Oral tradition of the other day's clumsy, lamentable venture. First they called it the Battle of Manosque. They said: The Manosque rebels held in check more than a thousand Germans who finally called on the help of the air force. Manosque brought down three planes! (with what no one says). The German soldiers had to take Manosque house by house, they were shooting through the windows, blood ran in streams!! The Germans then shot more than six hundred women. Oral tradition: A. Michel told me the story of Guy's adventure this morning, as told to him by Mme. Jalade.

Bonnet told me he was tortured for hours in Céreste and finally they marched him in front of a corpse, saying to him, "That's how you'll end up if you don't confess!" (Confess what?)

At lunch we were talking about the extraordinary names in this region. One especially: Exubis Abdon. Exubis is the family name. Like first names here: Marguery, Cather.

*Wednesday, June 28*

The sky bears fantastic castles of clouds. In the afternoon heat they bombard one another with an artillery of gold across lakes of pure blue. They collapse so very slowly; the debris takes all day to rumble down from the pinnacles of the towers to the shade of the forests that cover the gulfs at the foot of the walls. They collapse as slowly as men who sometimes take a hundred years to do so. Through gaps the sun bursts forth.

Beginning to work again.

A first name from the period of my youth. It was the brother of one of my father's workers, an epileptic. The one legend held to be a Zouave and who made dolls for me from the lids of the shoe polish. They cut my fingers like razors. After five minutes of playing with them (because they were very beautiful, in copper-colored tin as brilliant as gold), my fingers were all bloody and I ran off to cry in the darkness of the attic. I tried to leaf through the volumes of Alexandre Dumas in the big goatskin trunk and I got blood stains on *La Dame de Montsoreau* and *Vingt ans après*. The brother's name was Tallien. He's still alive. He's a farmer.

*Sunday, July 2*

Worked steadily all week.

Summer has arrived with relentless heat, sky hard and empty, very blue, very uniform, smooth, seamless, enclosing us perfectly.

The other night I tried to see friends. Except for Paul R. who is calm and natural, the others are crazy. G. sly and deceitful. Ludovic E. kind but evasive as water, and finally, A.Z., hysterical, nasty, bitter, fearful, and cruel. Horribly cruel and the one most influenced by the propaganda. An instrument of hatred. After that, I'll be very careful not to try again.

The revolution continues, without grandeur, murder of defenseless people under cover of darkness. I have no pity for those who die waging war. Henriot and the others. They are waging war, they know the risk they run, their deaths are normal and logical. But more and more, hatreds are despicably acted out. It's not a matter of saving one's country, it's a matter of establishing the authority of one political party and using the quickest means to arrive there, by murdering one's opponents. That's the sign of a vulgar idea.

Bernard's father, and then his wife, wrote to tell me of his death. Olga Fr. told me about the abandoned corpse lying in the road all day: by evening the bees had eaten the eyes!

*Monday, July 3*

Now when someone's opinion differs from yours, he doesn't try to convince you or even respect you, or imagine that maybe you could be right, no, he kills you. Times like those experienced by Piedmont and Lombardy in the period of the Condotterie. Florence in 1150. But today it's sadder and less chivalrous. The weapons are all on the same side. On the other side are only rabbits that can be shot *without any risk*. How glorious to kill this one or that one or some other one, there's no risk. There's no law and order, no distinctive weapons. These times without grandeur.

Read a few scenes from *Voyage en calèche* to Dr. Petit. Everything must be redone as I thought. Not to take anyone's opinion into account anymore, to be free as the wind, and to invent without a care. Now to get started.

Nothing more from Gide on Algiers radio. At least it can be said that he's not a hothead. Is he the kind of man not to get fired up when he encounters paradise?

From my window this evening, I'm watching my neighbor Maurel who's working in his garden. He's hoeing his rows of corn. He's the one, of course, who must rebuild the world. But it must be him, he himself, in person, and not his representative. He won't know how to delegate someone. He will know how to reconstruct the world, but he won't know how to send someone in his place. He will be fooled by the tricks of politics. I have faith in him, but none at all in the one he would choose.

Horribly difficult days, without joy and without hope. Much worse than my days in prison. No rest, no food. Nothing.

Nothing to delight either body or mind. Stripped of everything, I am working on *Deux cavaliers*.

Aunt Noémie has yet to die. Three weeks ago Élise and her mother went to see her. She was supposed to die then. Her debt's come due and she won't pay. It's like the saying goes: *She'd rather owe it to us her whole life than have us waste it*. And this despite the surgery.

*Friday, July 7*

Completely exhausted, I returned from the Criquet farm last night. It was ten o'clock, just at curfew. I rang the bell. Finally they could stop worrying. Élise came to the door at the same time as the children who opened it for me. She said nothing at first but greeted me tenderly and fiercely. As tired as I was, I didn't see her tears. A little later she said, "I'm going to tell you something that will cause you great pain." Then she said, "They killed Jean Bouvet." My dear Jean! Purity and peace. Killed by machine gun in Mâcon. Marthe wrote the very day it happened, June 27. We didn't receive the letter until yesterday. I still can't comprehend that it's true. Haunted all last night and all today by his voice, his gestures, his good smile behind his glasses. I can still feel his prickly beard when we embraced a year ago. I see him alive. I see him riddled with bullets, "drained of all his blood." Rotten world! Rotten men, dirty rotten men! Jean! No, I truly can't believe, can't comprehend it.

*Monday, July 10*

Horrible days, Friday and Saturday. Haunted by Jean Bouvet's death. I can see him as if he were still alive and I imagine the terrible murder, the appalling spectacle that Marthe and the children had to witness, and the grandmother. The first sentences of Marthe's letter, so beautiful, keep coming back to me and give me physical pain. The whole dependable, loyal soul of Jean Bouvet has disappeared. It's impossible to express the sadness of these two days. On Saturday Germaine Bellec came from Céreste, overwhelmed as well, her eyes full of tears. Thinking of her husband's death, too, in Mollans last year, she told me that she will no doubt end up as a believer because "it's not possible that everything is here." Oh yes, Germaine, everything is here. Everything is in this life. The truth is that there is no death. But as you mean it, yes, it exists. Egoistically for you, for us, yes, there is death. In the face of life, no, there is nothing; there is no opposite of life.

Sunday evening I was able to refocus on things a bit. Today I'm feeling better. I still haven't dared to work but I think it won't be long before I get back to the chapter in *Deux cavaliers* entitled "History of Arms."

Last Thursday the Germans shot two young men against the cemetery wall, eighteen to twenty years old, found carrying weapons.

Robert Berthoumieu had Jean Bouvet killed to save the lives of the Braumans.

*Wednesday, July 12*

This morning Élise woke me at six o'clock. Someone could be heard walking or rather wandering about upstairs in my office, above my bedroom. He was dragging his feet. At first we thought it was Guy doing who knows what. Guy sleeps in the bedroom next to my office. "What is he doing?" Élise asked me, "it sounds like an old man." I put on my clothes, about to go upstairs barefoot, but when I opened the bedroom door, there was Uncle coming down. He was barely conscious and couldn't speak. I took him by the hand and led him to the kitchen. I tried to understand him or make him understand me, but without success. He was still a bit responsive and tried a few times to explain something to me as well. I got Guy up and sent him for the doctor. Before the doctor arrived, Uncle had a glimmer of consciousness and heard and responded to me. The doctor drew blood from Uncle's arm. Then, as I was holding the basin I felt strange and I stepped out for air in the garden but I just had time to make it back to the terrace before I blacked out, stupidly. Still conscious, I heard the doctor say, "Lay him out flat, he'll come to in a minute," and I answered, "Yes, I'm alright," and I was. Sensitive and even squeamish. Why? Because of the blood? But that's stupid, I saw plenty of blood from 1914 to 1918. It's perfectly ridiculous.

Alert at ten-thirty. But this time we could hear the planes and suddenly the sound of two dull strikes farther away. Those were bombs on the Valensole plateau. We could see smoke rising and then a huge squadron, wings glistening in the sun against the blue sky. They went around Manosque, to the south. They were very high. Bombs on the plateau again, with tremendous smoke. I made the women go inside and stand against the main wall of the house. But I was reassured by the course the squadron took. It headed toward the southwest side of Pierrevert, where huge plumes of red smoke rose in the distance not long after.

This time they were bombing very close to us and from all sides. While we were eating lunch at one o'clock, enormous mushrooms of white smoke erupted from fifty kilometers south. At three o'clock, the postman told me that the countryside was burning southwest of Pertuis.

Uncle is still barely conscious but wanders stubbornly about the house nonstop. He doesn't recognize anyone anymore, except me, apparently. His pants are full of excrement and urine. He's covered with flies. There's no way to convince him to get undressed or to let us undress him and put him to bed. I must get him to the hospital, absolutely. We can't take care of him here.

Hundreds of times I've been called to come deal with Uncle, who can't keep still, goes into the garden, bangs his head against the wall and insists on wanting to go through it or remains rigid there as if he'd had a stroke. Hundreds of times he's listened to me. Then this evening when I was worrying about how to make him go to bed, he went up to his bedroom all by himself and began to get undressed. I was too upset after my queasiness that morning. I unlaced his shoes and pulled off his disgustingly soiled pants. Undressed and lying down, he looked at me with, it seemed, a bit of intelligence and tried to explain something that remains a total mystery. But I thanked him for thinking of me in that way. He was the plague of my father's life and for more than thirty years my own most serious worry, but this evening his look touched me.

It's very strange; at first it took a bit of effort to touch those soiled pants, but then I helped him out of them with less effort and disgust than I would have thought. It's easier than one imagines. Finally he's undressed and in bed. I only have to watch him one more night, and tomorrow I think that I'll move him to the hospital where he'll get more regular care.

*Thursday, July 13*

I've just taken Uncle to the clinic. They put in a catheter to discharge his bladder. There's no question that I was right to make this decision and to make it quickly. At home he can't be kept clean, he would have ended up cutting himself, getting an infection, and suffering. He might have had a bit of apprehension, if he understood, because his generation is afraid of hospitals (although he's at the clinic, not the hospital); I looked into his eyes to see if there was any anxiety. I was afraid of that. I pondered this a long time, but I'm sure that, without considering our interests, I've made the best possible decision on this matter, in his own interest.

*Saturday, July 15*

I've just come from seeing Uncle at the hospital. Yesterday he was able to say, "sit down." Today he could only pat my shoulder slowly with his hand. When I left he said goodbye to me with his hand. Suffering has given him a kind of tenderness to which I'm extremely sensitive. I take pleasure in going to see him each day. I brought him a bottle of good wine, a jar of jam, and some milk. He's not really such a bad fellow either, at heart. He wanted to play the braggart all his life. In the end he'll lack nothing, whatever he did. Suffering ennobles. He looks very beautiful with his beard.

Uncle destroyed my peace all my life, but he just gave me the greatest joy that anyone could give me: he had faith in me. When the attack came over him, with the little life and intelligence he had left, he immediately made his way to my office to find me. When I took his hand on the stairs, he followed me. Just a little while ago, he awkwardly tried to thank me. It was the most moving thank you I've ever received. And it's thanks to him that I've just now regained confidence in myself and the certainty that I'm right to forgive everything, and that I'm worth something. If I were to do nothing else in my life, it would not have been useless. In his unconscious distress, I represented to him help, salvation, protection from pain, from the mystery of his pain and fear of death. He was certain. That certainty moved me as never before. When he came to find me upstairs in my office at five in the morning, and when he didn't find me and stayed there pacing about until, asleep below him, I was finally awakened by his pacing, he had at last decided to come down without me. He was lost. I opened the door of my bedroom. He was in the stairway. He stopped and looked up toward the office where I should have been. I called him. He didn't hear me. He was still looking up, moaning, expecting to see me emerge from above. I took him by the hand. There, he said to himself, finally, there he is, and he followed me. I see his poor face again, the trail of saliva running down his beard, the extraordinary trust in me that overwhelms me; I may never in my life see a face more consoling to me than that one. I am repaid beyond all that he owes me.

*Monday, July 17*

I've just come from the hospital. They operated on Uncle this morning. I was there. Once more he looked at me. He is going to die. I am losing him like a beloved being.

*Tuesday, July 18*

Uncle died last evening at six o'clock.

*Wednesday, July 19*

Yesterday they arrested the gang that was committing masked, armed robberies under the guise of resistance. They would come to your house, sometimes even in broad daylight, search you, demand a few hundred thousand francs. In extreme circumstances they took checks that they made you cash for them at the bank, accompanying you there concealing a pistol. During this time, they held your wife, mother, or children to threaten you. Then they took off. The gang was arrested. There were thirty-five of them, including two policemen, two chauffeurs from the Grands

Travaux, and to everyone's astonishment, many classy, well-heeled, well-raised citizens of Manosque, "gentlemen."

Another thing. Another thing altogether. There's a rumor circulating that Martin-Bret was arrested, by the Germans. So a meeting could be held with the whole Oraison Resistance Committee.

There have been three days of oppressive heat, sad sun; without joy and without hope of joy. Uncle was buried this morning at ten o'clock. At nine-thirty I went back to the hospital where they had kept him. He was in a small chapel laid out stiff under muslin. His friend Raymond had made the coffin. It was also Raymond who, with the help of the hospital gardener, had laid Uncle in the casket. He had folded a sheet over him and propped him up with wood shavings. He had taken exquisite care to put shavings on either side of his head, densely packed, and he had flattened them with his hand so that they didn't fall onto his face. Uncle's blue eyes, closed when he died, were open again. He has come to look very much like his father, the Zouave. His hooked nose. Raymond is Uncle's old drinking companion. It was very beautiful the way he had (in his fashion) taken great care over the dead head. Everyone said to me that Uncle had a millionaire's funeral. They don't know the whole story, the last (last and first) moments of tenderness, and the hand that gently smoothed the pillow of wood shavings.

But behind the hearse, and crossing the market square, I really felt that, with regard to the life of the senses, all this sentimentality is a fool's game and that a poor man's life is worth more than a millionaire's funeral. And now under what magic sail does he navigate? A hundred billion times nearer the treasures than we are. Even if he is only matter, he is on the magic side of matter.

*July 29*

This evening, Champsaur, passing through on his way to Seyne to see his family, came to pay me a visit. He never fails to do so anytime he's passing through. I like Champsaur very much, for his intelligence, his heart, his qualities. His faithfulness to our friendship touches me deeply. I gave him a good explanation of *Les Grands chemins*. I should be able to write it as well as I explained it to him. How easy it is out loud. I must transfer that ease into the writing. (The idea of the cobwebs is good and the weapons that allow for his freedom at the end. Maybe he'll leave dying; maybe he'll take two more steps and then die, but he has left.) We'll see, it's an idea in any case. And it makes the book into something closed, constructed.

I returned to fishing yesterday. All day in the sun and in the sands of the Durance. I learned very quickly to gather up the line in my hand. In fact, I'm quite good at it. We caught three kilograms of fish, but with great difficulty. Toward evening the fishing was better, with fish being caught by the dozens, all very fine. Nothing but roaches. Not a single barbel. The other day in the same spot, nothing but barbels and five kilograms without any effort. I came back last evening completely exhausted. But I'm fine today, physically. Mentally, still very anxious, bouts of deep sadness, waves of dark despair, and then I regain strength, regain hope.

*August 1*

Having just come from the Contadour, Olga Fradisse brought me very bad news regarding Lucien's health. We fear for the worst, she told me. He's in terrible pain, believes it to be cancer. It might be only a stomach ulcer. Lucy Fr. who is a doctor and is up there with Olga claims that it might be nothing, but he should see a specialist. I told Olga to urge Lucien to listen to me. I'll make an appointment with Fernand Aviérinos in Marseille and Yves Bourdes, one of the best surgeons in France, I'll go to Marseille with Lucien, I'll take him by taxi. Down there he'll get the care he needs. "But," Olga said, "will he agree to abandon his garden?"

Bombs in the city, shattering the nights. Élise is afraid.

Determined to end this money crisis, I'm writing to Grasset and some Swiss publishers. I would like to avoid selling (manuscripts especially, or animals).

By working steadily, I can finish *Deux cavaliers* in three months. I not only can but must, now.

And I must also organize my solitude since it's going to last and it could devour me.

I think it'll be easy for me to write *Les Grands chemins*. The beginning would already be there if I could get started on it.

Beginning to read Balzac again. *La Rabouilleuse.* Even his exaggerations are true.


*August 2*

I haven't said anymore about the alerts. There were two between ten and one o'clock. During the last one, a squadron came from the north, passing right over the house. Earlier a squadron flew east-southwest in the direction of Avignon or Marseille. It is two o'clock. The alert remains in effect. Some people have just died. It makes the time purer, harder, the most luminous in the world.

Marthe has asked me for a few words to appear at the top of a small plaque in memory of Jean.

*Sunday, August 6*

An alert this morning at nine o'clock. At noon it still hasn't ended. Individual planes and large squadrons continuously roaring over. Rumbling on all sides, to the horizons.

Since his article, "The Emigrants are Always Wrong," I'm worried about Gide's fate in Algiers.

X wrote me that in Paris Maggie (Guiral-Vaudable) has begun to host lavish dinners with the future (probable) leaders of the Communist party as the guests of honor. Cocteau wriggling about among them. (Vaudable = Maxim's).

Last Sunday I heard that Martin-Bret and Picquemal might have been shot in the Baumettes prison in Marseille. I don't believe it. This news was reported to me by W. just as I was going to the movies. On Monday Curet told me the same thing. He doubts it as well, but badly wants to be well-informed.

Tormented by the desire to write *Les Grands chemins*. I must hurry up with *Deux cavaliers*. Hurry but not ruin it.

Still tired from the day of fishing on Friday, but a very healthy tiredness, my limbs happy and at peace.

Still no response to the letter that I wrote to Lucien. It may be difficult for us to take a taxi. What an agony for him, this trip to Marseille!

*Tuesday, August 8*

Wonderful shop signs: the cabinetmaker who had already posted on his door: *coffins, reduced prices*, has added something splendid: *blinds repaired*. In Paris, near the East station I noticed: *rendez-vous with gas* (at a bistro). In Taninges at a coffee merchant's: *Mont-Blanc roasting*. In Marseille, this epitome of the comical: *Hôtel de la Pompadour et du New-Vichy*.

Alert yesterday (it lasted three hours). Alert today.

I am organizing my solitude.

Last evening Crébely saw the chessboard set up on my little table. He taught me a few openings. Damiano defense for black. King's gambit versus queen's gambit. I proposed to him the king's gambit declined to which I countered the symmetrical king's gambit accepted. That didn't seem correct. We continued playing to see. Despite his expert knowledge of the game, he had a very hard time finally checkmating me after which I not only nearly nullified the game but even neatly recovered and attacked. The checkmate was very difficult and forced by the knights.

*Friday, August 11*

Again the legend of my "immense" fortune, my flatterers, my court, my "evolution" in a letter from J. Cousin d'Aubervilliers. I answered him with precise facts regarding the truth. In the end, this is all comical.

Yesterday fishing, a storm that caught us without shelter. Soaked to the skin. Protected a little by my waterproof jacket and hat, I gave my dry shirt to Gaston Pelous who is more delicate with his old lung abscesses; I gave him everything I had to cover himself and told him to run and dry off at the farm. Naked as worms, Blavette and I began to pull in the line and we caught some magnificent fish: barbels and roaches. In a little while, the sun came out again and dried us, but we were forced to remain naked until seven o'clock in the evening. Our worries about Gaston were over when he finally reappeared, warm and dry, with our dry clothes.

Work going well on *Deux cavaliers*. The rhythm of my solitude helps me.

*Sunday, August 13*

Three or four alerts yesterday. Today two alerts already before noon. But no noise in the sky, not a single plane. We end up no longer paying attention to the siren and no one can say anymore if the alert is beginning or ending. Opulent heat these days and dazzling light. A terrible peace. They say the Americans are at Rambouillet.

To smoke, I'm going directly to the garden to pick green tobacco leaves that I roast in the oven of the stove and then crush in my hands before filling my pipe. The smoke from them is overwhelming, bitter, strong, and immediately produces a kind of sickening vertigo. It makes your head swim. Very unpleasant. From time to time, Charles makes me a few grams of real tobacco with the same leaves that he cures with saltpeter and boiling water. Then I can smoke a few very good pipefuls, but I give so much away to all my friends that I quickly run out of it.

Read the famous *Judas* by Rabinovitch, which he worked on for two years and it's thirty-eight pages long. One thinks to oneself: thirty-eight pages, two years of work! Rabi is intelligent, this must be good. No. It's bad. It's not of the same order or measure. It's constipated. No interest whatsoever, neither human nor general. Small rage lacking grandeur. On the other hand, read some of Bellion's verse, the subprefect in Forcalquier, and it's very beautiful; full of rhythmic cadences, music, and beautiful, noble thoughts. Among the best of today's poetry. And he's written a collection of stories, also very beautiful, especially "The Pornographer."

Also read Maurice Chevaly's stories. Undeniable talent. Not enough discipline and work (self-sacrifice) yet, but talent.

I pass judgment, I'm getting old!

*Wednesday, August 16*

Second day of bombing here. Since Monday evening I haven't been able to write. Four killed by machine gun in Saint-Clément in a car, my neighbor Léonce Amalric among them, pierced by bullets, and then the next day my own adventure that I'll write down here one of these days if I have the time and peace for it.

Today they tried to demolish the bridge over the Durance with huge bombs that shook us four kilometers away. We've finished the shelter in the garden. My mother is holding up. Élise and Sylvie are happily at Margotte since Saturday evening. A very courageous attitude on the part of Aline who remains by my side and wants to stay here. She's helpful and shows herself to be level-headed, wise, and cool. We are waiting. No sleep last night. I'm sheltering a young cleaning woman with a little girl in the small house, a survivor from Toulon, very frightened. Wonderful weather. I went up to my office after lunch to write these few lines to regain my footing after the crazy upheavals of yesterday afternoon and a sleepless night; I am very sleepy. Played card games with André and Marcel. Everything is purely a question of luck.

*Thursday, August 17*

The time will come for the "*Joli Jésuite à la petite tache humide.*"
(Thomas Mann)

Fairly calm night. We slept. Early in the morning planes returned and dove over Saint-Tulles. Bombs fell near Corbières. After noon again four planes circling over the same spot and more big bombs dropped there. I don't see what the target can be at that spot. They haven't returned to bomb the bridge again. Not yet, at least (it's three o'clock in the afternoon). Huge fire near Valensole after the bombs dropped. Turin Dessaud came back from Margotte and brought me a letter from Élise and Sylvie. They are frightened up there. They bombed the Forcalquier viaduct near them and the Saint-Maime cemetery. I wrote back that under no circumstances should they leave there and I gave them a few orders to obey. Apart from dropping bombs, planes are machine-gunning the roads, a little randomly it seems. In short, at least so far, a calmer day than the last few, a calmer night.

Received a good letter from Lucien, who agrees to go to Marseille, but when, now?

A thunderstorm – a simple thunderstorm, enormous – arriving from the south.

All contact with Manosque has been cut off. We have only our neighbors. We're together more and more. Small patriarchal clusters are forming from house to house. The town is silent, still, all the stores closed except from six to eight in the morning.

The storm broke about six o'clock. It's not raining. But this dry thunderstorm is making more noise than the bombs.

There are fourteen dead at Vinon. The day before yesterday we saw our four usual planes that dive over and drop big bombs. Now we're used to these four planes returning periodically to bomb us. Turin has set off again with the letter for Élise. If things calm down a bit, I'll go see her with Aline. We'll go on foot. We'll go through the woods and stay the night. Let's hope for a calm night.

And fundamentally, what purpose does all this serve? Tuesday, when I was hiding under my olive tree, on the road along the pass, and when the plane with its machine gun was searching for me, circling like a bird of prey, what beneficial work was accomplished? What could that little cyclist, who had tossed aside his bike and run to take cover, truly represent? This wasn't the *joli jésuite*, it was the anthropoid. Ah, how convenient it is to consecrate the halberds on the altar of the fatherland, what a *black liberty* that provides.

*Friday, August 18*

The night was absolutely calm. Not a sound. It was delightful. The crickets were singing madly. It seemed like perfect peace, like a cool fountain. This morning too it seemed as though our misadventures were over. But about ten o'clock two planes arrived that were flying very low, at barely ten to fifteen meters, and circled over us. Then they headed upriver beyond the hills and we didn't hear them anymore. They swept over us again not long after, still flying low, and roared over Saint-Tulle, circling, gaining altitude, striking, then one of the two fell. I was watching them from my office window, I had a very good view of the falling plane. Its descent was preceded by a silent flash coming from the ground. Suddenly it burst into flame like a huge red mushroom. The other plane took off. If this was an attack by the machine gunners at the factory, we should expect retaliatory air strikes.

My mother is bearing everything very bravely, but this morning she was very short of breath.

I've stopped working on *Deux cavaliers*. I read. I listen and watch for planes. I keep an eye on the house, making sure that no one hangs the sheets out to dry, like yesterday. Make my mother come back inside at any sign of danger. I smoke the raw tobacco from the garden that Charles won't use anymore because the smoke ruins his lungs. I play cards with André and Marcel. Time passes very slowly.

*Saturday, August 19*

Yesterday, which I thought would be calm, was the most dangerous yet. I've even decided to evacuate my mother, mother-in-law, and Aline. At noon you could feel the fever in the air, then at twelve-thirty, eight planes flying right over the rooftops, directly above the house, dove and fired machine guns, and then for the first time, we could hear the hiss of bombs. This time it was very close. We learned afterwards that the station five hundred meters away was hit. In no time, the house has become like a refugee camp; Marcel and André arriving with their wives, then later Blavette and his wife. Quite distraught despite a bit of bragging. They'd gone for lunch to Mathieu's in the Prés neighborhood, a hundred meters from the station. The planes dove toward them and fired machine guns. They dropped the tomato salad they'd made and threw themselves on the ground. We spent the afternoon together, playing chess, cards, reading, smoking our horrible tobacco. Despite a few alerts for planes passing over, the rest of the afternoon was calm. About eight o'clock Blavette set out to leave, his wife broke down, and I suggested they sleep here. They agreed, happily. Blavette headed back to their house on the other side of town just to bring in the laundry and put away the leftovers of a mutton stew. But he returned shortly without having gone home, saying that the Americans are in Valensole (twenty kilometers) and that he saw (he repeated he *saw*) a pack of Camel cigarettes in the hands of a gendarme.

The night was calm; nothing but two or three low planes passing over.

This morning the French flag was flying from the top of the steeple and it's nearly official that the Americans are in Sisteron, La Brillane, and Oraison, that is, twenty-nine kilometers northeast, in the direction of Route Napoléon.

We are liberated.

Let us hope we are liberated from the bombings.

They announced the mobilization of men from eighteen to forty-five years old. Last evening the London radio station was praising a colonel, saying that he was, "a small manufacturer, great general, and handsome young man, thirty-three years old."

The plane that came down yesterday had hit some high-tension lines.

There's talk in veiled terms about a horrible bombing in Marseille that supposedly took place at the beginning of the week.

At eleven o'clock in the morning the Americans arrived. The town was buzzing like a hive. I heard little Renée crying, "Maman, come quickly, they're here!" I went to the window. An auto passed below on the road. It displayed a large tricolor flag. The eleven o'clock bells.

I'm going to begin writing *Deux cavaliers* again, the next part, and finish the book. Then launch into *Les Grands chemins*.

Below in the meadow, the children are playing with a tricolor flag. Renée is waving it, then she clutches it by the fabric like a stick and chases the little boys, striking them on the head with it.

False alarm. What we took for the Americans was simply a car with flags. They say the Americans are now passing through Digne.

This afternoon I'll go see Élise at Margotte.

Blavette, invited last evening to lunch today, has arrived. The town is jubilant, it seems. They killed Mathieu the clockmaker because he was a double agent apparently, and Fayet the bailiff because he was the bailiff. Town gossip.

I have to give up on going to Margotte. The roads are overrun with young men shooting their machine guns at random. Add to that the fact that they're all completely drunk, and I really do think it's safer to give up and wait until tomorrow.

I'm spending my afternoon making a huge pot of pistou soup for this evening (green beans, garlic, oil, basil).

Marcel and André arrived late in the day. They were taking part in the celebration. As a militant Communist, André shares the secrets of the powers that be. He told me that Fayet was killed (or nearly, he's in a coma) simply by hitching a ride behind a truck, hanging on from his bicycle, and that no one shot Mathieu at all. I believe him. It's more Manosquean than the other version. They've simply arrested twelve or thirteen people. André is out of money and work. I lent him 500 francs. Last night I lent 500 francs to Blavette who's in the same situation. And I'm in the same situation. I have 20,000 francs total, that's all.

*Sunday, August 20*

The difference in views and desires between the majority of the population and the dynamic Communist minority established itself from the very first day. Last evening already the town became disenchanted after chanting all day. In the opinion of Blavette and of Charles Fiedler at dinner, people had suddenly become nervous faced with the initiative of the Communist backers. Then there's also this mobilization announced for tomorrow for all men between eighteen and forty-five years old. The Russian Communist Revolution of 1917 was directed *against* the army and against the war. What made it successful is that it immediately declared "the war is over." For the moment, people take comfort in saying, "it will be over soon now." But what if it's our bad luck that it's not "over soon"? This morning the bells rang for mass *timidly*. Differences as well between the F.F.I. and the civilian fighters. And the sensible people who would like everything to rest on solid foundations are suddenly shocked by the disarray of this army of deserters (I use that word simply to indicate that the Maquis groups were formed by men who *refused* the draft. One imagines that they refused out of patriotism; that was the case for a few of them; for the majority, it was simple selfishness, perhaps even fear). Yesterday there were displays worthy of the army of Toussaint Louverture and Soulouque. Blavette told of the parodic arrival of an auto, coming from Volx, packed with drunk, half-naked young men, draped with cartridge belts, wearing battered American helmets, entering Manosque with their machine guns aimed at the crowd. They were imitating the Krauts, they said. Everyone headed for the café where they were greeted with cheers and kisses by the women. They left again shortly, climbing into the auto like clowns on a carnival float, but so drunk now that, when the car shifted into gear, those who were standing and had assumed the stance of defiant wounded heroes tumbled onto one whose machine gun was aimed at the crowd. It's just by luck that a hundred people weren't killed. Debauchery in cars and on motorcycles, all backfiring. They've finally found their *unique* reason for being alive. All day long they've done nothing but mindlessly circle the town, going up and down the Avenue de la Gare, driving through the boulevards over and over. They have gasoline! Posted on the walls: *The Americans will guarantee each French citizen 2,000 calories a day!* This line is repeated in hushed tones, discussed, everyone's already stuffed to the gills! What magnificent happiness: 2,000 calories! The Perrin-Langevin-Brauman return! There they are with their laboratories slung over their shoulders. What a good life they're going to make for us!

We can hear heavy gunfire in the direction of Aix, sometimes so close and so loud it shakes the windowpanes.

Durieux's son came to thank me for the help and shelter I gave him as a resister. And I have an explanation for the bombing that we're hearing. An armored division of Germans leaving from Cavaillon is heading toward Manosque, and there's fighting in Pertuis and in Apt. (Just now I was told there's fighting at the Granons crossroads, eight kilometers away.) Durieux was appalled by the mobilization order. Ludovic Eyries arrived, telling me about all his passive defensive maneuvers and strategies for avoiding danger. The whole time from lunch until about four o'clock, gunfire dully shook the country, sometimes close, then distant, then near at hand. André and Marcel are nervous, also appalled by this mobilization that terrifies them. They've taken down the French flag from the Saint-Sauveur steeple. And they've had all the flags along the streets removed. What a change since yesterday. How quickly the atmosphere of political conflict returns.

*Monday, August 21*

Rising early to visit Élise at Margotte, I see American infantry passing, heading toward Volx in trucks.

In town, bugles sound for reveille, meals, general salutes, saluting the flag, whatever, not to salute the Americans who passed through very quickly in the end (five or six cars at most) but out of military vainglory. Everything is military these days, despite the fact that everyone individually is trembling over the mobilization or else seeking the most cowardly ways to avoid it.

*Tuesday, August 22*

I finally succeeded in going to see Élise at Margotte. When I arrived in my sandals that make no noise, Sylvie gave a shout. She saw me on the doorstep and cried, "Papa!" and we all three embraced. At the Mort d'Imbert pass, there was a sentry. A man in a sailor jacket and jersey sitting on a bank by the road surrounded by an arsenal of rifles, machine guns, revolvers, and grenades. He watched us pass and said hello. Three kilometers on we were stopped by miners from Saint-Maime blocking the road. They asked us for our identity papers and let us pass. (I was with Marcel.) Coming back we were examined closely but cheerfully at three roadblocks. At the second, someone said, "Oh, you're Giono from Manosque, okay." At the third roadblock at the pass, some young men came rushing down the mountain when they saw us arrive. But at close range, one of them said to me as I was reaching in my pocket for my papers, "No, I know you, go ahead through, it's fine." The whole country was thick with the smoke from a huge fire in the direction of Pertuis. The rumbling of gunfire continued. We arrived in Manosque and near the cemetery we saw two Americans. They're in Manosque. They were coming through all day long in large numbers.

In the evening Maurice Chevaly came to see me. He's disgusted by the recanters. Farelacci, for example, who was vice-president of the Legion and now walks around shouting and gesturing in uniform and boots despite the horrible August heat, a thick white cord adorning his collar. His wife runs about wailing *La Marseillaise* and accosts Americans, dragging them to their house and their dinner table. He also told me about Julien Léon who has decked himself out with the two-barred Cross of Loraine; Signoret who putters about on his motorcycle with the resisters that he fought; the Aubert family, formerly of the Croix-de-Feu, Legionnaires, you name it, now parading around with their chests stuck out, braids and embroidered flags on their sleeves. Regarding the alert of two days ago when a German armored division coming from Cavaillon reached Manosque, Maurice Chevaly said, "If you could have seen those cowards fighting over the flags and garlands, decking themselves out at top speed." I told him that the real game is being played in the back rooms and this noisy masquerade will very quickly be supplanted by the first brutalities of the real poker party. He told me that a local Liberation Committee has been named representing the National Council. Vital Besson, a Communist, is president. This committee has four members, two of whom are Communists, among them Camoin, my daughter's English teacher, with whom I'm doing the translations of Fielding's *Joseph Andrews*.

Someone called this afternoon, apparently, from the Café Glacier; someone wants to see me. Who?

I'm not leaving the house and not going into town. It would be difficult for me not to say what I have said. I'm hearing rumors.

Back from his night of so-called heroic guard duty, Guy says that he passed his time simply riding his motorcycle around the Valensole plateau. They brought home tobacco and American food items. They can only be called *items*. These are synthetic products: Dextrose tablets, chemical products, pastilles, citric acid flakes to replace lemon. Everyone plays greedily with all that. But today, one American soldier, having filled his helmet with fresh carrots, was eating them hungrily as though a gift from the gods. Here we're tired of gifts from the gods. How appealing these laboratory products are! To remain an honest man. I'm taking advantage of these idyllic times by reading *L'Astrée*. It's good. Sometimes it's like Stendhal – how strange – despite the difference in style.

Just to note that fear over the mobilization continues. We all reassure one another that it's a long way off, that there are no uniforms, no barracks, and in the end, who knows? But everyone is talking about it, everyone says, "No, they couldn't, it's impossible, reassure me, I'm telling you, I have no desire to be mobilized."

The mobilization order is signed *Édouard*. Neither first nor fourteenth, *Éduoard*, that's it.

Blavette brought me an American. He's Spanish and lives in Los Angeles. Don Juan Rafael Lopez. I gave him a copy of *The Song of the World*, which he wanted. He gave me his pen (with which I'm writing). Then Don Juan pulled out four medals from his wallet and arranged them, three on the right and one on the left.

The telephone call yesterday was an American from the photography division of the army who says he's read all my books and would like to meet. He speaks perfect French. I told him to come whenever he likes. He said to me, "How extraordinary it is to hear your voice."

A huge cloud of wine-colored smoke from the direction of Marseille, which they say is burning.

*Wednesday, August 23*

The American who called came last evening at nine o'clock. His name is Freddy, he says, and he brought two others with him, Sidney and Gordon. I think that he's claiming to be called Freddy because clearly he's French and Jewish. He speaks better French than English and at one point whispered to me that he wanted to speak in French slang to me to explain that he did not like America very much. That surprised me. He saw it. The three soldiers are part of the photography division of the Army. With Freddy acting as interpreter between Gordon and me, they questioned me about the future of France. They are pessimistic. I am, too. Gordon wants to do an article on our conversation for *The New Yorker*. They stayed until midnight and we're going to see each other again today.

Wustner who accompanied the Americans to my house said, "If anyone bothers you, let me know." He has, he says, "heard talk." I tell him that I wish everyone had done as much as I did for the poor wretches hunted down by the Gestapo, the Jews (Meyerowitz, Lévine, Mme. Ernst), as well as the Communists (Charles Fiedler), as well as the resisters (Francis Dessaud, Roger-Paul Bernard, Durieux, the two Bonnefoy boys, Jules de Cavaillon). The first refuge for resisters in the Basses-Alpes was with me at the Contadour. They stayed there for several months, until the dispute with Lucien. And I forgot to mention the Fradisse sisters, and I forgot everything else I did. We'll see if they forget, too (which is what I expect anyway). And I've forgotten André. The smoke from the fires entirely covers the whole country. Any slight movement of air is like the hot breath of an oven. Turmoil. Noises, cries. Cheering, endless explosions. Toward evening the smoke turns blue and wine-colored and settles heavily. There must be fighting near Aix.

Chess games with Blavette. I won one of them.

Oh, Tibet! If I can, I'll go spend part of the winter in the mountains. Near Valgaudemar. To have cold, and solitude and silence! What a prospect of happiness, it seems unreal and unrealizable.

*Sunday, August 27*

It's been a few days since I've written anything in this journal. I note in it my mood at the time in the face of events, sometimes hour by hour, always at the very moment. On-the-spot. Nothing is meant to be read. It's my self-portrait; it's not a portrait of events. This allows me simply to gain my footing, not to be pulled under. Friday they arrested Aubert, Brel, Guérin and many others, fourteen in all, I believe. This morning a parade of the "resisters" in town at the monument to the dead, salutes to the flag. From my house I could hear them singing "*La Madelon*." At noon my two cousins André and Marcel arrived and ate lunch here. They're sporting tricolor cockades and their Communism is very military. This afternoon Camoin came to see me. It seems that Fluchère is the big boss of Information. They're all preparing violently and in good faith to shed their illusions. They've already made a good start. Camoin talked to me about the political games that everyone has already begun to play. Noting that Y. brought them files of denunciations. But he had the courage to sign them. Which, Camoin said, is rare. Because he also said that anonymous denunciations are pouring in. And he added that after turning in his files, Y. went to offer his legal services to the Guérin family. Basically he seems quite disgusted by all this.

It's hot. Terrible heat, stifling and La Nauséeting.

Decided to begin work again first thing tomorrow. Finish *Deux cavaliers*, then immediately begin *Les Grands chemins*.

Blavette brought an American here who sells tobacco and chocolate, which I did, in fact, buy, tobacco for my pipe and strange, chemical-tasting chocolate for the children. Élise returned from Margotte yesterday with half a bucket of butter that isn't real butter and doesn't melt in the pan. It hardens and sticks. Everything has a horrible laboratory taste. Everyone delights in it and swears to high heaven they've never eaten anything so good. Perfect.

Last evening, trucks full of German prisoners passed through Manosque to booing and hissing. I don't like that. Such outbursts lack nobility and dignity. We won't create a "beautiful France" with feelings like these. When I say this to Blavette and André, they laugh smugly or try to outdo one another, telling me about alleged offenses that the prisoners supposedly committed. I say "alleged" because the "cutting-off-the-hands-of-children" myths are circulating again. They are broadcast to justify our little acts of cowardice. A great country has other responses.

*Monday, August 28*

Dr. Petit came to see me as he does every Monday morning. I gave him a bit of American tobacco and two tablespoons of that strange butter that doesn't melt. He said, "Yesterday I went to the 'procession.'" He said, "At the hospital I'm caring for a German with eye wounds. I'm doing all I can so that he won't go blind. How beautiful my profession is!"

Began to write again this morning. Two pages of *Deux cavaliers*.

*Tuesday, August 29*

Excessive heat. The air is unbreathable. 38 then 39 and then 40 degrees in the shade. Stifling wind from the south. My mother is truly suffering. I'm forcing myself to work in my office, which is hot as an oven. The country noisy, the sun overpowering, the air thick, the land appearing entirely reddish and burnt, the light dazzling, all too much. My only recourse is work. Wrote three good pages of *Deux cavaliers* this morning. I'm beginning to read Proust again. Also the letters to Trébutien from Barbey d'Aurevilly; also Saint-Simon's *Mémoires*, and from time to time a little of *L'Astrée*. I keep cool thinking of autumn and then winter, wonderful winter, imagining that maybe I'll be able to spend some time in the mountains, maybe even by myself. Putting my hopes in work alone, and if there's more ahead for me, so much the better. And if that's all I'm left with, it's worth something nonetheless.

Crébely stopped by again last evening, as is his habit every Monday evening. Analyzed a Winawer-Steinetz chess game with him. At a certain point I experienced an intense sensation of pure classical beauty. This morning he sent his wife over with the analysis of the center gambit declined that we had discussed last night, Alekhine versus X.

At about four o'clock the heat is unbearable here. I'm sweating standing still, not moving. I open the shutters a bit. The sky is chalk white. The light wind barely stirring the linden leaves is burning hot. Across the valley, in the meadow, I see men lined up (about thirty of them) and I hear an order: Present arms! I also hear the gunshots of those doing target practice. I must recognize and admit that I was wrong to believe in pacifism. It wasn't made for man. War must be exalted. Then you "get respect." Because it's deeply human. It's what everyone demands and desires. When there are huge massacres, don't be outraged, be content with polite expressions for the survivors. Make use of the "most common of commonplaces" like: I offer you my deepest sympathy. Don't forget the *deepest*. Make a sad little face (that's enough), and move on to something else. That's the perfect attitude for winning the highest regard. At fifty years old, with these very simple precepts, you can attain the reputation of a perfect gentleman; you can be at ease anywhere and peacefully enjoy everything.

Manosque, or the Nietzschean bourgeois.

"I have long favored reviving such games in France; a nation's tone is maintained by bloody spectacles."

Marquis de Sade (Juliette)

*Wednesday, August 30*

Last evening about six o'clock, Joffre Dumazedier came to visit.

He was at officer training school in Uriage (thus field marshall training); now an official representative, he's going from Grenoble to Toulouse in a car protected by machine guns. He stopped in Manosque to see me. He said to me, "Your actions lower you," that's the expression. I have no interest in that. He said, "Explain this to me: I've been told that you wrote to the Marshal of France and said that you wanted victory for the Germans." I answered, "Think for a minute. If I'd written to the Marshall (supposedly to praise his farm policy – which contradicts my actual actions, for example, defending the farmers around Margotte, as I've noted earlier here), if I'd written to the Marshall, you would have *seen* evidence of that writing. Reviews like *France*, on the look-out for anything that could help Vichy propaganda, would have reported on such letters, rest assured. Have you seen anything even resembling that? No. So? Draw your own conclusions. Someone told you that I said, etc. To whom did I say it? Did they give you details so that you had grounds to believe it, or do you believe such things simply because it's easy and pleasing to believe bad things you hear about those you're used to admiring?" He admitted it. I added that I never wanted to be admired and that I wrote in *Le Poids du ciel*: "I write neither to be loved nor to be followed, I write so that all readers can decide for themselves." Decide for yourself with precise and proven facts. You can see very well that these aren't that. He admitted this as well. I quickly laid out for him my activities during the occupation: coming to the aid of individuals in need, Jews, resisters, and Communists. I cited names, I gave evidence. He shook my hand and left. That was all.

This morning the French army came, heading toward Grenoble. A lieutenant with the tanks, Michel Lemaignand, stopped his column on the road and came to see me to shake my hand. This combatant is brighter, sharper. A good exchange of ideas lasting two hours. We're entirely in agreement.

Increasingly unbearable heat. It borders on torture. Racked by the light, heat, and noise. No rest anywhere. I long for the mountains, cold, winter, peace, dark days, silence, and physical joys in keeping with the heart. The heart is degraded without joys. The nobility of physical pleasure. What there is of it seems only to diminish.

Reading is truly the sensual pleasure of uncertain times. Hence the success of the literary arts in the Middle Ages. Never has Proust been so vivid, so poetic, from so powerful a magic source as with this reading that I'm doing now, tortured by the noise of passing armies and mass delirium. As though there weren't enough natural baseness, a public notice advises, demands, charges us to denounce, even anonymously, those in the ancien régime. That's going to be a beautiful sight.

Wrote two good pages of *Deux cavaliers.*

Eight o'clock at night. For the first time in a long time, I've just heard a train whistle! I'm leaning out the window. Yes, there it is, it's coming, there's smoke. Soon there'll be mail, I hope.

*Thursday, August 31*

Visit from Effantin. He's the garage mechanic from Lalley with whom I took walks in the mountains eight years ago. I introduced him to Gide who played a game of chess with him, I wrote about it in my journal at the time. Gide lost and afterward had a very beautiful chessboard sent to Effantin. He just drove a big shot to Saint-Tropez. He's part of an F.F.I. group. He told me, "You were often attacked in front of me. I defended you every time. I said, 'I know him; he can't possibly be other than what I know him to be.'" (There it is. Plain and simple.) He smiled and when he asked me if I remembered our walks in the mountains, I told him, "Yes," and I added, "With you the mountains were twice as beautiful. It was a joy to hear you speak." This man who has simply retained his trust in me does me much good. What a difference from Joffre Dumazedier, not bad either, but a quibbler. It's true that Dumazedier *did not know me*. If that's all it takes, it's very flattering to me. And frankly, just between us, I actually believe that *is* all it takes. Knowing me is enough. (What arrogance, they'll say. Well, why not, since it's the truth, why not be proud of that? Is it so common?)

Unbearable heat. Tortured by physical desires and needs.

Effantin told me about the French soldiers' animosity toward the Americans (Lemaignand had said the same thing). In Saint-Tropez, he said, women don't dare go out alone anymore and barricade themselves in their houses. He added that the big shot he drove was going there to counter Russian influence. It's more likely that good Effantin doesn't know his big shot's real mission. I'm noting briefly what he told me to help describe the present confusion in people's minds and thinking.

I've read all of Proust carefully at least ten times. This time re-reading *Du côté de chez Swan*, I realized for the first time that I was locating Combray in Normandy while it must be located, I believe, between Riems and Laon. Of course that's because I first read *À l'ombre des jeunes filles en fleurs*, with the first location, as everyone else did. The trace of Balbec has not yet disappeared. The book gains in leafy shadows, as Combray seems near Shakespeare's Arden. It's easier to understand the Guermantes.


*Wednesday, September 5*

I haven't written anything more here for eight days. I began again yesterday and I numbered these pages beginning with 1. New events have taken place that I'm going to try to note down beginning from today. This is still, now more than ever, my self-portrait, and if Joyce hadn't already used the title, it would be, precisely, the *Portrait de l'artiste par lui-même* that I'm writing. First of all, for the last eight days, I've continued to read Proust and in large doses since I've read *Du côté de chez Swan* and *À l'ombre des jeunes filles*. Today I'm beginning *La Prisonnière*. Also read a little of *L'Astrée* and last evening took up *Don Quixote* again, which has suddenly penetrated me very deeply, as it does each time, similar to embers in ice. Played chess and even began a game long distance with Crébely, each of us playing one move per day. Yesterday, played a Knight B8 – C6 (black), a waiting move that threw him off. Remained stretched out on my divan, reading, waiting. A very difficult week. It takes hellish strength of character to wait patiently as I have done. Also read one hundred pages of Saint-Simon and glanced over Retz today, which I'm certainly going to try starting again. Meant to continue with Machiavelli several times but I haven't taken up reading it again. The weather shifted suddenly from hot to cold; from 39° in the shade yesterday to 16° today. It rained a little. Today the sky is overcast and the humid air delights me. I still don't want to begin the account of the events of these past eight days. Below my windows, endless convoys rumbling along the road. There's fighting in Briançon, which the Germans had supposedly retaken. For the first time in eight days, I have a little calm and rest. I'm waiting for Guy to return from Marseille where I sent him yesterday morning with a letter for Henri Fluchère. But already I have some peace and I can see clearly.

Had a visit from Lévine yesterday. He told me he was an intelligence agent for the F.F.I. He thanked me for all the help I gave him every time he was hunted down. I never gave it a thought; he was being pursued and needed help. He's going to Marseille today, he told me, to denounce those who had denounced him. "What a pleasure," he said, "I'm free to get behind the wheel of a car again."

The road rumbles as though lashed by the tail of a furious dragon.

There are trucks full of Arabs, Indo-Chinese, and Annamites passing through.

A fine autumn taking shape, rich, indolent, and melancholy. The trees in the valley have turned a dark and heavy green, and despite breaks of sunshine, the sky is dark, as I like it.

*Thursday, September 6*

It was just eight days ago, last Thursday evening while Chevaly was visiting, that Mme. Wustner's arrival was announced. I asked Chevaly to let me receive her. He went downstairs to wait in the library. Mme. Wustner came up. She was very upset and her distress confirmed the fears that I felt instinctively as soon as she was announced. She stammered out that I was going to be arrested. Her husband had heard it at the F.F.I. headquarters. It was, apparently, the Republic Commissioner, Aubrac, who said in passing that he was surprised I hadn't been arrested yet. "Giono," he said, "hasn't he already been arrested? What are you waiting for?" Indignation from Wustner who wants to hand in his resignation and immediately he sent his wife to warn me. At the time, this left me almost indifferent. I thanked and gently dismissed Mme. Wustner, reassuring her, and I had Chevaly come back up, calmly ending our visit. When he left, I saw the difficulty, the difficulties for my mother and Élise. The trouble of being subject to humiliation by our entire lunatic population, seething like milk. This is clearly no picnic. I'm certainly not afraid of the National Security Committee. On the contrary, it might let me make public my real actions during the occupation. I imagine it's very easy to compile all the facts, all perfectly and easily verifiable, that will leave these gentleman flabbergasted. And what a surprise when the facts are compared to the legend! The reassuring part is that everything is perfectly verifiable through testimony, and that testimony comes from witnesses impossible to suspect. Thinking this out, I went down to dinner and said nothing to anyone. But the next day was the funeral for Aunt Noémie, who finally died from her "intestinal eclosion," and to explain why I couldn't go to the funeral I had to break the news to Élise. She took it very bravely. I waited all morning, and then for the rest of the day, and nothing happened. At this point, I've decided to make the first move. What purpose will it serve for me to sit around, who knows how long, in the Digne prison, especially with people on the other side; according to hearsay, ten or twelve per cell, and simple thin soup once a day. Nevertheless I've accepted the idea without enormous dread. I know that even there I can experience great joys. But it's unbearable to wait. Every time the bell rings, I say, "There they are." Each time, no, and then the waiting begins again. So I've made a summary of those *verifiable facts* and, after calling Curet who's agreed to defend me, I've delivered the summary to him so that he can use it to build my defense.

Ah, it's raining, the sky is dark, low, soft as down, and the rain is drowning the distances in milk; it's so cool that I've put on a sweater. The leaves stand out against the dark trees. What peace! Over the course of the morning, the rain has become more and more wonderful. There's hardly any daylight here. The foliage on the chestnut trees is singing loudly. Hedges shimmering in the silver rain emerge from the distance in the valley. And above all, this delicious moist air, cool and thick, that lubricates the whole body. But sadly the wind is from the north. What wonderful charcoal clouds amassing in the south.

Retz, who delights me this time, a little *L'Astrée*, a little *Don Quixote*, Stendhal's letters (1825, so rich, Divan VI), sometimes Saint-Simon who remains dry (sometimes crystalline, but sometimes arid) (especially after reading Retz, so rich, so similar to the present times). And what else: I'm mixing in old volumes of the *Tour du monde* dating from 1868, a very fat study on the utopian novel in English literature, so that's my reading for now. I've abandoned Proust.

For the last three weeks all sorts of cheering along the road below. They've exhausted all the patriotic songs. Right now there are troops going by, just letting out shrill, wild shrieks. I'm told that these are Moroccan Goumiers.

The clouds are breaking up. The rain has stopped. There are blue holes in the sky through which sunlight passes. But the south remains charcoal and the west is heavy with that good melancholy of autumn. Will life return with its hopes and its peaceful joys? Oh, to feel distant once again from all struggle, from all politics, my only ambition to enjoy each day, enjoy life.

Sunlight about five o'clock, from the west where it's completely clear now.

Ludovic Eyriès came to see me, to chat, and he brought me the latest news from town. Little by little I'll discuss it. Basically, he was nervous, his pale eyes darting about. He came to ask my advice. I gave it to him.

Still haven't resumed work on *Deux cavaliers*. I've just been writing this journal, my self-portrait. But on my table lies the page interrupted eight days ago. And maybe tomorrow – thank heavens – I'll be able to start working again.

The whole sky this evening swept clean and bright. The western horizon sleek and clean as a sword. The rain is already over. It's cool, but it's the rain that I love, the thick, moist air and the sound of rain in the gutters and the trees. It is so peaceful.

More than ever I need solitude, mountains, silence, and peace. Nothing that I see can make me love man and society, and the empty hustle and bustle of enterprises that devour energy and strength for nothing. Nothing they create is of value. For me, in any case, I would be completely happy in a mountain hut on the most solitary Valguademar peak. Kilometers away from anything civilized, newspaper, radio, anything like that.

L.E.'s remark, not so stupid after all, speaking of B: "They can keep you from thinking, if they want to." You said it!

On September 8, 1944, two days after the last journal entry, Giono was arrested and imprisoned for collaborating with the enemy. Although no charges were ever brought, he was not released until February 1945.